THE
HIDDEN PLACES

of
The Lake District
and
Cumbria

SECOND EDITION

Acknowledgements

This book would not have been compiled without the dedicated help of the following : -
Elaine & Adele ,Administration ,Albert, Les , & Sarah, Artists
Bob,Jody,Simon,Harvey,Gerald ,Jim ,Clare, & Debbie, Research
Hattie & Jennie Writing & Production ,and finally , Alice, .editing .

OTHER TITLES IN THIS SERIES

The Hidden Places of East Anglia
The Hidden Places of Somerset, Avon & Dorset
The Hidden Places of Southern & Central Scotland
The Hidden Places of Notts, Derby & Lincolnshire
The Hidden Places of the Thames & Chilterns
The Hidden Places of Northumberland & Durham
The Hidden Places of Gloucestershire & Wiltshire
The Hidden Places of Hampshire & Isle of Wight
The Hidden Places of Lancashire & Cheshire
The Hidden Places of Hereford & Worcester
The Hidden Places of Devon & Cornwall
The Hidden Places of Yorkshire & Humberside
The Hidden Places of the South East

Printed and bound by Guernsey Press Channel Islands
©M & M PUBLISHING LTD
Tryfan House, Warwick Drive, Hale, Altrincham, Cheshire. WA15 9EA

Introduction

THE HIDDEN PLACES is designed to be an easily used book, taking you, in this instance, on a gentle meander through the beautiful countryside of the Lake District & Cumbria. However, our books cover many counties and will eventually encompass the whole of the United Kingdom. We have combined descriptions of the well-known and enduring tourist attractions with those more secluded and as yet little known venues, easy to miss unless you know exactly where you are going.

We include hotels, inns, restaurants, various types of accommodation, historic houses, museums, gardens and general attractions throughout this fascinating area, together with our research on the local history. For each attraction there is a line drawing and a brief description of the services offered. A map at the beginning of each chapter shows you each area, with many charming line drawings of the places we found on our journey.

We do not include firm prices or award merits. We merely wish to point out *The Hidden Places* that hopefully will improve your holiday or business trip and tempt you to return. The places featured in this book will we are sure, be pleased if you mention that it was *The Hidden Places* which prompted you to visit.

THE HIDDEN PLACES
OF
Cumbria

CONTENTS

Kendal and the Cumbrian Dales

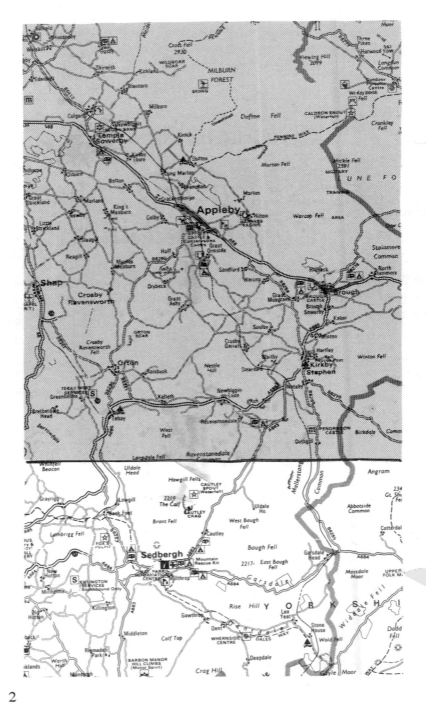

2

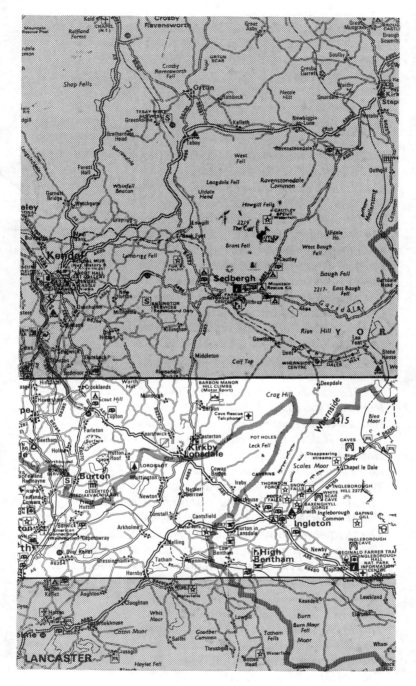

CHAPTER ONE

Index

Webbs Garden Centre, Burneside Road, Kendal
The Wheatsheaf Hotel and Inn, Brigsteer, Nr. Kendal
Winmaur B&B, 90 Windermere Road, Kendal
Woodclose Caravan Park, Casterton, Kirkby Lonsdale

Kendal and the Cumbrian Dales

Barbon Beck

CHAPTER ONE

Kendal and the Cumbrian Dales

The ancient town of **Kendal**, in the valley of the River Kent, was once one of the most important woollen textile centres of Northern England. The Kendal woollen industry was founded in 1331 by one John Kemp, a Flemish weaver. It flourished and sustained the town for almost 600 years until the development of competition from the huge West Riding mills in the Industrial Revolution of the 19th century.

The town was also famous for its Kendal Bowmen, skilled archers clad in Kendal Green cloth, whose longbows were made from local yew trees on the nearby limestone crags. It was these men who fought so decisively against the Scots at the Battle of Flodden Field in 1513.

Kendal has royal connections too. Katherine Parr, the last of Henry VIII's six wives, lived at Kendal Castle in the 16th century before she became Queen of England. Today its ruins, high on a hill overlooking the town, locate one of the original Roman camps that guarded the route to the Scottish Border.

Mason's Arms   Kendal   0539 724200

Kendal, the largest town in the old county of Westmorland, has always been a bustling town, from the days when it was on the main route to

7

Scotland. Nowadays the M6 and the Kendal by-pass divert much of the traffic away from the town centre, but its narrow main streets, Highgate, Stramongate and Stricklandgate, are still busy, and the fine stage-coaching inns of the 17th and 18th century, to which Bonnie Prince Charlie is said to have retreated after his abortive 1745 rebellion, still line these streets.

One such inn, on Stramongate, is the **Mason's Arms**, built in 1730. It is full of character, set in three tiers with a wood panelled bar and wall in the top area and comfortable, old fashioned seating in all the bars. Run by Ken and Mary Beck, it has been updated to provide modern comforts whilst still retaining its original charm and appeal. There are excellent ales available as well as a wide choice of bar meals, all served in a friendly, relaxing atmosphere. Should visitors wish to stay, there are five well-equipped letting bedrooms available, with uneven floors merely adding to the character of the establishment.

Kendal

Another distinctive feature of the historic centre is the series of named or numbered 'yards', tucked away down alleyways and through arches, once the focus of local small industry. Walking down Highgate their intriguing, narrow entrances are irresistible to anyone with a sense of curiosity.

On Stricklandgate the **Sawyers Arms** is a friendly, old-fashioned pub, run by Jane and Malcolm Heap.Its warm, welcoming atmosphere is immediately obvious, and has locals and tourists happily swapping tales over a pint of fine ale. At lunchtime there are sandwiches available at the bar, and for those who wish to stay, bed and breakfast accommodation is provided. Available all year round, the rooms range from single to family size, and all are spacious, clean and comfortable. Whether or not you decide to stay, The Sawyers Arms is well worth a visit whenever you are in Kendal (Tel: 0539 729737).

Da Franco's   Kendal   0539 722430

Stricklandgate runs past the Town Hall, which still houses Katherine Parr's Book of Devotions, and turns into Highgate, where regular visitors to Kendal will probably head for **Da Franco's Restaurant**. Established for 18 years, it is a first class Italian restaurant, candlelit and full of atmosphere, with a varied and reasonably priced menu to suit all tastes. More recently the proprietor, Franco Messina, has added Da Franco's Albergo dei Lagi, "The Hotel near the Lakes". It offers superb accommodation in the form of a 2-bedroomed penthouse suite, 2 family, 5 double or twin, 2 twin and one single rooms, all excellently fitted out with en-suite bath or shower and colour TV.

The Moon   Kendal   0539 729254

A little further along Highgate is **The Moon Restaurant**, run by Val MacConnell. Originally built in 1790, it is a very informal no-smoking restaurant which provides first class homemade vegetarian, meat and fish dishes. The menu includes international as well as English cuisine, prepared with flair by Val and her assistant chef Sharon Moreton. Above the restaurant there is a cosy room nicknamed 'over the Moon' where smoking is allowed and you can enjoy a pre-dinner drink or after dinner coffee. On the first Tuesday of every month you can book in for Sharon's pudding club, where you can learn the secrets to such delights as chocolate tia maria squidge cake!

While you're on Highgate, look into the **Brewery Arts Centre**, which combines a theatre, with an excellent programme of touring productions, an art gallery and a cafe. At the bottom of Highgate is the **Abbot Hall Museum of Lakeland Life and Industry**, themed around traditional rural trades of the region, such as blacksmiths' or wheelwrights' work-shops, agricultural activity, weaving and printing. There are re-created cottage interiors and elegantly furnished period rooms. Abbot Hall Art Gallery forms part of a complex within Abbot Hall Park and includes work by John Ruskin and the celebrated Kendal painter, George Romney.

Adjacent to Abbot Hall is the 13th century Parish Church of Kendal, one of the largest in England with five aisles and a peel of ten bells.

Kendal Parish Church

Facing the Town Hall, Allhallows Lane leads to a road known as Beast Banks, which climbs steeply to **Hillside Guest House**. The road was given its name when local people used to tether their "beasts" on the green near to the Guest House, before going on into Kendal. Carl and Brenda Denison have been providing bed and breakfast accommodation for nearly twenty years, and their experience shows in their six spacious letting rooms, four of which are en-suite, and all well decorated, providing the most modern facilities. These factors combined with a good town centre location, friendly atmosphere and hearty breakfast, make Hillside Guest House a lovely place to stay.

Hillside Guest House   Kendal   0539 722836

Kendal is a good centre from which to explore South Cumbria. There is good railway and motorway access and some surprisingly nice walks from the town, along the River Kent or into the surrounding limestone hills. It is this stone that gives the buildings the distinctive, pale grey colour which is such a familiar characteristic of the Lake District.

A few minutes from the centre of Kendal on Windermere Road you will find **'Winmaur'**, a first class bed and breakfast establishment run by Win and Mo Robinson. Set back from the road, there is ample parking space at the front of the house, and to the rear are marvellous views towards The Heights and Serpentine Woods. Once inside, the friendly, welcoming atmosphere is immediately apparent and you will soon find yourself relaxing. Mo and Win have been providing bed and breakfast accommodation for fifteen years and their experience shows. There are three very tastefully decorated bedrooms all en-suite and with colour TV and hot drinks facilities to ensure complete comfort during your stay.

Winmaur   Kendal   0539 720253

Further along Windermere Road, **Gateside Farm**, a traditional Lakeland farm, with beef, sheep and dairy cows, was built in 1680 and is run by June and William Ellis. Its situation at the Gateway to the Lakes makes it an ideal location for walkers and cyclists alike. William has lived here all his life, and he and June provide a warm, and friendly atmosphere for their bed and breakfast guests. Open all year apart from Christmas and New Year, they have five letting rooms all attractively decorated, with modern facilities including washbasin, colour TV, central heating and hot drinks facilities. In addition to a large farmhouse breakfast, June provides an evening meal five nights a week.

Gateside Farm   Kendal   0539 722036

Heading north-east out of Kendal town centre towards Tebay on the A685, a right turn will take you onto Fowl Ing Lane, not especially appealing from the main road, but worth following to an oasis of peace and tranquility at **The Garden House Hotel**.

The Garden House Hotel   Kendal   0539 731131

Standing in magnificent gardens, The Garden House is the epitome of

12

a country house hotel. The superb accommodation comprises ten en-suite bedrooms, some with four-poster bed, and all with the facilities you would expect. There is an elegantly furnished guest lounge, and the restaurant and conservatory with its beautiful mural, provide a charming setting in which to dine. The quality of the extensive A la Carte and Table d'Hote menus is commensurate with the surroundings, making The Garden House Hotel a truly first class establishment.

Cumbria Crystal

Continuing along the A685 the scenery changes quite suddenly to open fields and hillsides, and eventually the road comes to the village of **Grayrigg**, where a cluster of alms houses, cottages and a simple church form a lovely rural setting. This was the birthplace of Francis Howgill, 1610-69, who introduced George Fox to the Westmorland 'Seekers', a group of radical Christians from the area. Their meeting led directly to the establishment of the Quaker Church, the Society of Friends.

Grayrigg Hall   Kendal   0539 84689

Just past the church, a little turning to the left takes you to **Grayrigg Hall**, an impressive 18th Century stone farmhouse set in 1300 acres of

13

this splendid countryside. A working beef and sheep farm, it is run by the Bindloss family who offer two first class letting rooms, one family and one double. Jean has spent the last 8 years providing bed and breakfast for numerous visitors, and you can be sure of a warm welcome and comfortable farmhouse atmosphere. There is a substantial breakfast awaiting you each morning, and with prior arrangement an evening meal can be provided.

As a touring base for the Lake District, Yorkshire Dales and Moors, Grayrigg is ideal. Back on the main road again, **Punchbowl House** is a large Victorian stone-built farmhouse, situated in the centre of Grayrigg village. Built in 1877 it was formerly the working Punchbowl Farm. It is a non-smoking establishment run by Ian and Dagmar Johnson, who provide first class accommodation, comprising two double bedrooms, one en-suite, and one twin. All are centrally heated and have beverage making facilities and colour TV. The impressive dining room is beautifully decorated, as is the comfortable guest lounge, and walkers are well catered for with full drying facilities available. In an adjoining annexe which has its own entrance, there is self-catering accommodation, which sleeps up to six. Registered with the English Tourist Board, the bed and breakfast accommodation has been given a two crown rating and designated "Commended", the self-catering three keys and "Highly Commended.

Punchbowl House   Grayrigg   0539 84345

Near to Grayrigg is the litttle village of **Patton**, in a peaceful, rural location only four miles from Kendal. **Field End Barns** in Patton are tastefully converted farm buildings which form five excellent holiday homes all of which hold the ETB four key commended classification. These spacious and well-equipped houses are ideal for family or group holidays and their location makes them particularly safe for small

14

children with the nearest road being 1/3 of a mile away. There are many beautiful walks literally on your doorstep and fishing and horse riding are available within a mile. A mobile shop calls once a week providing most essentials and the milkman delivers three times a week. For a holiday at your own pace in idyllic surroundings, Field End Barns is ideal.

Field End Barns   Patton   0539 824220

If you leave Kendal heading towards the nearby village of Burneside, the **Oddfellows Arms** on Burneside Road is just a five minute walk from the town centre. Known locally as "Oddy's", it is run by Barbara and Geoff Wilson who came here two years ago and completely renovated the place. Originally two houses, it became a pub in the late 19th Century and still maintains old-fashioned, traditional values. It is immediately apparent that this is a place where people of all ages get together for a chat as they have done for the past 100 years. The piano in the corner proves a big attraction, with good old-fashioned knees-ups and singalongs of an evening. The pub is open all day every day, except Sunday, and lunchtime bar snacks are available, which on a fine day can be enjoyed in the pretty beer garden at the rear.

The Oddfellows Arms   Kendal   0539 722459

15

From here it is just a short walk to **Webbs Garden Centre**. This 3 acre site has a vast selection of plants, shrubs, trees and more besides. Originally set up in 1810 by a nurseryman called James Meldrum, the business was bought from him in the mid 1800s by Clarence Webb and has stayed in the Webb family to this day. It was Clarence who back in the late 1800s introduced the now internationally acclaimed Webbs Wonderful lettuce renowned for its crisp heart, and in 1922 James Webb developed a growing area for what became his award-winning varieties of dahlias and chrysanthemums. Later, James' son Geoffrey took over the business and moved it to its present site on Burneside Road where it is now a thriving business run by Geoffrey's daughter Judith and her husband Bill Stocker.

Webbs Garden Centre   Kendal   0539 720068

Open 7 days a week, Webbs Garden Centre has a friendly atmosphere and a knowledgeable and helpful team of staff to ensure you get whatever you need. The layout of the centre also makes it easily accessible for the disabled. The House Plant section is a delight, with a rich variety of both common and lesser known plants, whilst outside you will find an extensive conifer rearing area, and rows of rhododendrons, rose bushes, raspberry canes and fruit trees. Back inside the main building you can't miss the vast array of awards which virtually cover one wall, an indication of Webb Garden Centre's successes over the past 100 years. The centre's recent extension houses a selection of quality garden furniture and barbecue equipment. whilst in the lovely pine panelled restaurant you can relax and enjoy a tasty home-made snack. As you prepare to leave, you will doubtless be drawn to the gift shop which is full of tempting items which make perfect mementoes of a lovely day out, and from October to December there is the added attraction of an extensive Christmas display.

Garnett House   Burneside   0539 724542

A couple of miles along this road from Kendal brings you to **Burne-side**. There have been settlements here since the Stone Age, as is reflected by the remains of a stone circle on Potter Fell. By the 15th century Burneside was a settled agricultural area. A rich variety of mills sprang up along the River Sprint - fulling, corn, cotton, wool, bobbin and the original rag paper mill at Cowan Head.

Garnett House, run by Sylvia Beaty, dates back to the 15th century, and has been carefully restored to provide a high standard of accommodation yet retaining the age and character of the original building. There is a comfortable guest lounge with oak beams and exceptionally thick walls lined with 16th Century oak panelling, where visitors can relax in front of the television or enjoy a game of cards. In the dining room the emphasis is on wholesome farmhouse fare, with a full English breakfast and a five-course dinner provided. For those who prefer it, Sylvia also offers self-catering accommodation at Staveley, near Windermere.

Riverbank House   Garnett Bridge   0539 83254

Continuing upstream of Burneside, in 18 acres of beautiful country-side at the foot of the spectacular Longsleddale Valley, **Riverbank House** is a peaceful, homely establishment run by Julia Thom. Situated 4 miles outside Kendal, on the Westmorland Heritage Walk, the house enjoys an idyllic location with the River Sprint running alongside it, and in season it is possible to see salmon jumping upstream. There are three letting bedrooms, all tastefully decorated and with lovely views of the surrounding countryside. As well as providing a first class breakfast, Julia is happy to make up a packed lunch for her guests if required.

On the south side of Kendal, set back from Milnthorpe Road, is the **Headlands Private Hotel**, owned and run by Kate and Paul Coulter. Inside you will find a comfortable guest lounge with a small bar, a spacious, comfortable dining area, and seven beautifully decorated bedrooms. Four of the bedrooms are en-suite and all of them have the usual facilities you would expect from an establishment of this calibre. As well as breakfast, Kate also caters for evening meals if required, and will prepare a packed lunch on request. There is also off-road parking, which any regular visitors to Kendal will agree is essential.

The Headlands Private Hotel   Kendal   0539 720424

A right turn off the main Milnthorpe Road will bring you to the little hamlet of **Brigsteer**, about three miles away from Kendal between the parishes of Levens and Helsington. Snugly settled under the limestone escarpment of Scout Scar, Brigsteer is a very pretty village right off the beaten track and its focal point, beside a lovely beck, is **The Wheatsheaf Hotel**, a charming, traditional 17th Century inn. Run by Alice Harrison for the past four years, visitors are immediately welcomed into a warm and friendly atmosphere. There is a wide selection of fine ales available and a first class menu which boasts five starters and over 16 main courses, including home-baked chicken pie, beef curry, and duck a l'orange. With its traditional inn atmosphere and character, the Wheatsheaf is a lovely place to stay, and Alice provides cosy accommodation in three well-decorated letting rooms.

The Wheatsheaf Hotel   Brigsteer   05395 68254

Also in Brigsteer, surrounded by 15 acres of unspoilt countryside in the Lyth Valley, **Low Plain Farm** is a delightful 19th Century farmhouse owned by Jenny and Bob Arber, who provide first class bed and breakfast facilities. There are three letting rooms available, all tastefully decorated to offer individual and cosy accommodation. The farm has a comfortable guest lounge with colour TV, and a separate guest dining room where visitors can enjoy the wholesome breakfast that Jenny provides each morning, with an evening meal available if required.

Low Plain Farm   Brigsteer   05395 68323

Low Plain Farm also incorporates a Farm Park where you will find many different farm animals wherever you walk, some of them rare and minority breeds. There are various types of sheep, including the four-

19

horned, spotted Jacob, which is one of the oldest breeds, dating back to Biblical times. There are also numerous goats, with old favourites such as the silky coated Angora. Children will particularly enjoy the small animals corner, where they will encounter rabbits, guinea pigs and the like, and may even be able to give a lamb or kid its bottle of milk. Strolling around the Park, you will meet friendly donkeys, Highland cattle and ornamental pheasant. The Park is full of farm machinery from a Bygone era including many original Ferguson tractors and equipment. If you are feeling a little weary, you can pop into the Hay Barn where light refreshments are served, and where there are several static displays to look at, full of information about varying aspects of farm life, such as what goes into producing animal feed. Finally, you can browse around the well-stocked gift shop where you may well be tempted to purchase a little memento of your visit to this fascinating farm.

From the middle of Brigsteer follow the road which begins at the Wheatsheaf, into Brigsteer Wood. The climate is milder than Helsington and other nearby villages, perhaps because of its sheltered position, shown by the fine early flowering gardens and the prolific daffodils, early orchids, lily of the valley and other wild flowers in the Wood. The road will bring you to the village of Levens, on the southern tip of Scout Scar, overlooking the Lyth Valley and the lower reaches of the River Kent. Here you must see Levens Hall and its unique Topiary Garden.

Levens Hall

The Elizabethan mansion developed from a 13th century pele tower and the garden was laid out in 1692. Levens Hall is said to be haunted by three ghosts, a black dog, a lady in pink and a gypsy woman who, legend has it, put a curse on the family saying that they would have no heir until the River Kent ceased to flow and a white fawn was born in the Park. In fact after many years without a direct heir, in 1895 the River Kent froze over and a white fawn was born too, and a son and heir was born.

The neighbouring village of **Sizergh** has its share of similar tales. At Sizergh Castle, an impressive National Trust estate, the ghost of the Lady of the Castle in medieval times is said to haunt the Castle screaming to be released from the room that her fiercely jealous husband locked her in and where she starved to death while he was away in battle.

The Strickland Arms   Sizergh   05395 60239

The Strickland Arms, a traditional Victorian inn at the gate of Sizergh Castle, is also owned by the National Trust. It is a charming building overlooking a large, well-kept beer garden. Inside the atmosphere is warm and welcoming, with a good selection of fine ales and excellent food. Gill and Peter Muschamp who run the inn provide a variety of daily bar snacks, plus a set weekend menu in the restaurant. The set meals offer excellent value with three choices of starter and at least three main courses each day, whilst the restaurant itself is reminiscent of a grand drawing room, being cosy, intimate and welcoming. Once a month the Muschamps have a "themed" evening, with appropriate food and atmosphere supplied. Ranging from Italian, Spanish and other foreign evenings, to the occasional Country and Western night, these make a popular attraction of this charming inn.

From the main gate to Sizergh Castle, you will see a sign to the **Barn Shop and Tearoom**. These are fairly recent additions to **Low Sizergh Farm**, a working dairy farm which stands in 275 acres of lovely

Cumbrian countryside an area which is the source of much of the produce on sale in the Barn Shop. Set within a 17th Century Westmorland stone barn, the ground floor of the shop offers fresh farm made dairy produce including real cream dairy ice cream, cheese, butter, fresh vegetables (some organic), preserves and pickles, many using traditional Cumbrian recipes. Fresh strawberries are available when in season, or you may pick your own. Upstairs is a veritable Pandora's box, with crafts of every description, many produced by local artists. To complete your visit, pause awhile in the charming rustic tearoom which overlooks the milking parlour, and sample the freshly ground coffee, Lakeland tea, home-made light lunches and mouthwatering freshly baked farmhouse cakes, pies and scones on offer.

Barn Shop and Tearooms   Sizergh   05395 604326

A pleasant journey towards Kirkby Lonsdale can be made from here by taking the back lanes passing quiet villages such as Sedgwick and Stainton, until you join the A65 at its junction with the M6. On this road is the village of Lupton and **Green Lane End Farm**, a charming stone-built farmhouse standing within a 150 acre working dairy farm in a peaceful, secluded location. Pat and Robert Nicholson have been providing bed and breakfast here for nearly 15 years and visitors will find a house full of character. There is a magnificent wooden staircase leading to the spacious yet cosy guest rooms, and an excellent farmhouse breakfast is provided each morning. For those who prefer self-catering, the Nicholsons also have two well-equipped 2-bedroom apartments available to let at Mill Brow House in nearby Kirkby Lonsdale. About four miles west of Kirkby Lonsdale, away from the busy main road, is **Hutton Roof**. This is a village of great charm - stone cottages with a little Victorian church close to the limestone pavement known as Hutton Roof Crags.

The old town of **Kirkby Lonsdale**, on the banks of the River Lune

Green Lane End Farm   Kirkby Lonsdale   05395 67236

(hence its name), is almost on the edge of the Yorkshire Dales National Park. Despite the conflict of allegiances, this town has maintained its character over the years, and as it is set well back from the main A65 road, it remains a very traditional, handsome market town, where life still revolves around the market place and its 600 year old cross. Lovely Georgian buildings crowd along the winding main street and there are interesting alleyways and courtyards to explore with good shops to browse in, delicious bakeries and some wonderful tea shops. **Nutters**, in the market square, is a favourite for really good food, a very cheerful atmosphere and the best cup of coffee for miles.

The view from the churchyard is delightful, extending over the valley of the Lune to the fells beyond. JMW Turner was inspired to paint this very scene and John Ruskin wrote enthusiastically to write about what he saw - *"The Valley of the Lune at Kirkby Lonsdale is one of the loveliest scenes in England..."*. Since then, the name Ruskin's View has stuck.

Hesketh Newmarket

The arched bridge over the River Lune below the town, Devil's Bridge, is reputed to be at least 600 years old, and got its name from the legend of an old woman who, unable to cross the deep river with her cattle, asked the devil to build her a bridge. He duly did this in return for the soul of the first creature to cross. But the clever woman threw a stick across the bridge which was collected by her dog, cheating the devil of a human soul, and he disappears with a howl of rage, leaving behind his neck collar which some say can still be seen in the river below.

Woodclose Caravan Park   Casterton   05242 71403

Off the A65, close to Devil's Bridge, is a particularly pretty caravan park. Owned by Mr and Mrs Short, **Woodclose Caravan Park** extends to six acres just 300 yards from the River Lune, and, although only half a mile from Kirkby Lonsdale, the site is very quiet and peaceful. Woodclose has privately-owned static vans and is licensed to take tourers and campers, but there is a lot of space and no overcrowding. Formerly run by Mrs Short's parents, the family have been at Woodclose for 30 years, and have fostered a relaxing atmosphere of friendliness and homeliness. The facilities are of a very high standard and include showers, a laundry and shop, a public telephone and a play-area for children. Electric hook-ups are provided for touring vans, Calor-gas is stocked and milk is delivered daily.

Hipping Hall   Cowan Bridge   05242 71187

A little further along the A65 towards Skipton, is the village of **Cowan's Bridge** and **Hipping Hall**, a 17th century country house set in 4 acres of lush walled gardens. Inside it is elegantly furnished, and there is a warm, friendly atmosphere. The spacious dining room has exposed rafters and a polished wooden floor, with a large table where guests dine together. The first class, five course dinner is served by the proprietors, Ian Bryant and Jocelyn Ruffle, with appropriate accompanying wines. Jocelyn offers an excellent set menu which changes daily and is prepared using home and local produce. The accommodation is of an equally high standard, with five double bedrooms all with private facilities and colour TV, whilst in addition there are two cottage apartments available for bed and breakfast or self-catering.

The drive from Kirkby Lonsdale to Sedburgh, on the A683 which follows the River Lune upstream, is quite beautiful. The river forms the geographic western boundary of the Yorkshire Dales National Park, a gentle valley on the edge of fertile farmland and rolling hills. Shortly after leaving Kirkby Lonsdale, you will come to **Casterton**, a pretty village of grey stone cottages and a church with a remarkable collection of Victorian paintings by Henry Holiday and James Clark. The village is perhaps best known for its Girls Boarding School which has links with the Brontes.

The Pheasant Inn   Casterton   05242 71230

The **Pheasant Inn** at Casterton is a picturesque, country hotel offering its visitors excellent accommodation amidst beautiful scenery. The facilities are first class with ten en-suite bedrooms, including one four-poster, all individually furnished to a very high standard and well-equipped, including colour TV and direct dial telephone. There is charming residents' lounge in which to relax as well as a garden lounge which is reserved for adults, and designated a no-smoking area. In the bar guests are welcomed by cheerful staff who can offer a range of hand-pulled ales and selection of excellent bar meals. There is also a beautiful panelled restaurant which offers an outstanding menu using freshly prepared local produce, accompanied by a high quality wine list.

The Middleton Fells Inn   Middleton   05396 20258

Further along the same road, just beyond Barbon, is the **Middleton Inn**, known locally as 'The Head'. Built in approximately 1650, it has been completely refurbished by the owners, Sandra and John O'Neill, but still retains its charm and character. It is very popular locally which is probably due to the first class ales and tasty bar meals which are on offer every lunchtime and evening. There is an extensive range of daily blackboard specials, as well as a set menu, a special Sunday lunch, and children's meals. Outside on fine days customers can enjoy the large beer garden and excellent children's play area.

The views on the A65 to Sedburgh are spectacular, but it is worth taking some of the side roads on the way to explore some of the villages and walks right on the Yorkshire Dales border.

The Sportsman's Inn   Dent   05875 282

Leave the main road at the little village of **Barbon**, shortly after Casterton, and travel up Barbondale and past the wooded estate of Barbon Park into Dentdale, to Dent, the only village in one of Cumbria's finest vales. **Dent** has a delightful cobbled main street with tall cottages where the famous *terrible knitters* of Dent produced stockings and gloves for sale at Kendal Market. A fountain of pinkish Shap granite in the village centre indicates Dent's links with Professor Adam Sedgwick, 1785-1853. Woodwardian Professor of Geology at Cambridge University, Sedgwick was one of the greatest field geologists of all time. He never forgot his native dale and wrote a moving account of the valley as it had been in his childhood.

There is much to explore here and plenty of beautiful walks. In the neighbouring hamlet of Cowgill, **The Sportsman's Inn**, beautifully refurbished and now a listed building, is an ideal base for walking, caving and potholing. There are five double rooms and one family room, all situated at the front of the Inn with lovely views of the River Dee that runs through Dentdale, and the Settle to Carlisle railway line. Sandra and Ron Martin, the proprietors, supply excellent hand-pumped traditional ales and mouthwatering home-cooked food. There is a good hike for the stalwart walker, from Lea Yeat to Great Knoutberry Hill, along part of the old drovers road, or for those who prefer to travel by car, the picturesque market town of Hawes is only a short drive away.

A.S.

High Hall Rare Breeds Farm   Dent   05875 331

Animal lovers will appreciate the concept of **High Hall Rare Breeds Farm** in Dent. Run by two charming and devoted ladies, Sheila Tickle and Cynthia Bailey, the farm is home to numerous breeds of cattle, goats, pigs and sheep, all threatened with extinction. High Hall is acknowledged as the oldest building in Dent, having a history of almost a thousand years. Set in 211 acres of beautiful countryside, it is an ideal site for a rare breeds haven, which is what it is. The farm was opened for visits at Easter 1989, but is continually developing, and a special interest corner has been set up, housing several rare breeds of farm dogs, donkeys, ponies and shire horses. High Hall is indeed a rare place in itself.

Dent Crafts Centre and Hop Bine Restaurant Dent   05875 400

Situated approximately one mile out of Dent towards Sedbergh is the **Dent Crafts Centre and Hop Bine Restaurant**. The Centre is housed within a traditional Dales Barn, which was originally built during the late 17th Century. Run by Louise Hunt, Tricia and Brian Jones, the Centre has something for everyone, with a vast selection of arts and crafts, ranging from paintings and photographs, to pottery and jewellery. Throughout the year there are regular demonstrations of various crafts, such as lacemaking, wood carving, calligraphy, sugar craft, and green wood turning, to name but a few! The Hop Bine Restaurant is full of character with its flagstoned floors and beams. A non-smoking establishment, it has a varied and imaginative menu and has facilities for small children. Once a month there is a musical themed evening, with appropriate music and a menu to match.

Sophie's Wild Woollens   Dent   05875 323

Don't leave Dent without visiting **Sophie's Wild Woollens**, a shop and workshop where visitors can marvel at the extensive range of knitwear created by Sophie Schellenberg. All items are individually made and hand finished, (with even the buttons being homemade), and incorporate a host of imaginative designs and motifs to suit all tastes and ages. The workshop is on view within the shop, so you can watch Sophie at work whilst you browse through the mixture of fun jumpers, decorative tops, and warm hugging jackets. In addition to her own creations, Sophie also sells many other arts and crafts, including locally made jewellery, pottery, and aromatherapy oils.

The little valley winds past old farms and hamlets to **Lea Yeat** where a steep lane hairpins up to Dent station, almost five miles outside Dent. This is a marvellous place to begin a ramble into Dentdale or over the Whernside. Dent is the highest railway station in Britain, over 1100 ft above sea level, and is on the route of the famous Settle-Carlisle Railway line.

Dent street scene

Just north of Dentdale is **Garsdale**, both a dale and a village, over-looked by the dramatic Baugh Fell. The Clough River follows the dale

Sizergh Castle

from Garsdale Head, the watershed into Wensleydale, where a row of Midland Railway cottages lies alongside the former junction station on the Settle-Carlisle line. This is now a surprisingle busy little railhead where the steam locomotives, occasionally used on the line, pause to take water from a moorland spring.

Garsdale Foot Farm   Garsdale   05396 21329

From the village the A684 follows the course of Garsdale into Sedburgh. On the way, **Garsdale Foot Farm**, set high up within the boundaries of the Yorkshire Dales National Park, probably has some of the finest views in the area. Built in 1790 and owned by Wendy and Phil Willoughby, it offers two spacious and beautifully decorated letting rooms. The restaurant seats up to fourteen and oozes elegance and style. For anyone booking a table, a menu is sent to them in advance, so that their choice of starter and main course is already prepared. The choice and quality of the menu reflects the class of the surroundings, making it an ideal venue for an intimate dinner for two, that special celebration, or just a well-deserved treat.

Sedbergh is a town of subtle character, set in countryside of outstanding beauty. An old market town with cobbled streets, it is dwarfed by some of Alfred Wainwright's favourite fells, the mighty Howgills, Firbank Fells and Baugh Fell. It is Sedburgh's location in the midst of this striking scenery that has made it such a thriving community for hundreds of years, at the confluence of four valleys and four rivers where ancient trade routes merged. The market dates back as far as the 13th century.

On Main Street the **Dalesman Country Inn** is exactly what its name suggests, a traditional country inn. With its exposed beams, stone interior walls, and central fireplace with a welcoming log fire, it exudes a warm, friendly ambience. There are fine traditional ales available with the occasional guest beer, and an enticing restaurant known as The Buttery.

Here you can enjoy a family meal out or a cosy dinner for two, sampling tasty fare such as Wings of Fire, Japanese Prawns or Chicken Goujons to start, followed by the likes of Roasted Half Duckling, Hot Under the Collar (10oz sirloin steak covered in a tasty peppered sauce), or Local Lamb Chops. Every Sunday lunchtime and evening there is also Roast Topside of Beef, which is worth passing a few pubs for! If you have any room left, there is also a wide selection of desserts. In addition to the restaurant menu, there is a wide range of Dalesman Pizzas available, which you can eat in or take away. The accommodation comprises five bedrooms, three en-suite, and all excellently equipped with colour TV, hot drinks facilities, and most usefully, an iron and ironing board. There is also accommodation available, in the form of Dales Cottage, a small cottage about 1/3 of a mile from The Dalesman, with one double and one single room. It is small, but cosy and offers the same facilities as The Dalesman, and guests still have breakfast at the Inn. This is a favourite watering hole for cyclists as the **Cumbria Cycle Way** passes its front door.

The Dalesman Country Inn   Sedbergh   05396 21183

The Posthorn, also on Main Street, has changed very little since it was the Kings Arms Staging Inn, way back in the last century. Now it is a magnificent tearoom and restaurant run by Alan and Chris Clowes. It is a place full of character and warmth, with wooden floors, quaint tables and chairs, and to complete the ambience, lovely Bertie Wooster style music playing in the background. The Posthorn offers a wide selection of speciality teas and coffees, as well as a varied and reasonably priced menu. This ranges from toasted sandwiches, to all-day breakfasts or the substantial Coachman's Grill, a platter that includes steak, cumberland sausage, gammon and black pudding. There are also various appetising home-made cakes and you can even order jam roly-poly and custard!

32

The Posthorn   Sedbergh   05396 21389

Another Main Street coaching inn is the **Bull Hotel**, now owned by Harry, Margaret, John and Hazel Wilkinson. An impressive black-and-white timbered building, the Bull has played an important role in the life of this town . The cobbled street in front of the hotel makes it easy to imagine the noon stagecoach pulling in for refreshments! An excellent choice of delicious homemade dishes is available at lunchtimes and in the evenings, in portions ample enough to satisfy the hungriest visitor. There are also fifteen bedrooms, of which six are en-suite, a reception room and a guest lounge. Bed and breakfast, with or without evening meal, is available, and the welcome will be just as friendly as at the Craven Heifer and Mason's Arms in Ingleton, Yorkshire, the Wilkinsons' previous establishments.

Bull Hotel   Sedbergh   05396 20264

Just out of the centre of Sedbergh is **Farfield Country Guest House**. Set in 2 acres of gardens, it was originally built in the 1840's for a local

33

mill owner. Now run by Peter and Liz Newsham, it has seven well-equipped and tastefully furnished bedrooms, some en-suite, all with outstanding views. There is an attractive dining room and two lounges, one with a log fire for chillier evenings. In addition there are two self-catering units available. One is a lovely, well-furnished bungalow attached to the main house which sleeps two, the other is a static, mains connected 26-foot caravan, which sleeps two to four.

Farfield Country Guest House   Sedbergh   05396 20537

Nearby **Holme Farm** is a traditional dales working farm which opens to visitors daily from March 1st to 30th September, and the rest of the year by appointment. John Metcalfe and his son David run the 90 acre farm, which has several different breeds of cattle in the herd of suckler cows, and various sheep, pigs, goats and poultry roaming the land. There is a delightful nature trail one mile long with a protected badger sett and fox holes, which covers about 70 acres and takes from 1 1/2 to 2 hours to complete, longer if you decide to fish or picnic by the river. Visitors are encouraged to hold, stroke and even feed the young animals, and can observe sheep dogs working, milking, also sheap-shearing and lambing in the right season. Guided tours are given daily which include a chat about the animals and the farming system. Groups and school parties are welcome. Educational information including topic webb and work sheets are supplied. Evening tours concluding with a badger watch can be arranged almost any evening.

This area is filled with Quaker history. In the Firbank Fells Firbank Knott can be said to be the birthplace of Quakerism for it was here, in 1652, that the visionary George Fox gave his great sermon to inspire over a thousand 'seekers' from the whole of the North of England. This was to lead to the development of the Quaker movement. If you take the little lane which runs along the back of Firbank Fell , about half a mile west of the B6357, you can walk up to Fox's Pulpit, a simple boulder marked with a plaque just a short way from the roadside, where George Fox delivered his momentous words.

Holme Farm   Sedbergh   05396 20654

At **Brigflatts**, just off the A683 to the south of Sedburgh and a lovely riverside and field walk from the town. Here, close to where Fox stayed overnight with his friend Richard Robinson, is one of the oldest Quaker meeting houses in the world, a beautiful, simple building where Friends met for communal worship.

The Howgill Fells, a series of magnificent, open hills, most of them ancient common-land, provide some of the most spectacular countryside in the North of England for the dedicated hill-walker. Several tracks and old green-ways lead across them but you can also wander over the open summits, making your way to such peaks as Uldale Head, Yarlside and The Calf, at 2219 ft the highest point in the Howgills. The most spectacular feature of the Howgills is Cautley Crag, a great cliff several hundred feet high, alongside which a beautiful narrow waterfall, Cautley Spout, tumbles.

The Cross Keys Hotel   Cautley   05396 20284

Experienced walkers can reach the waterfall from The Calf but for most people it is more easily reached from the footpath that leads from **The Cross Keys**, a 17th century inn which is now a temperance hotel. Here is a place for the real lover of good food and a wonderful surprise for people who have never been before. It is owned by The National Trust, tiny and very old, not sophisticated, but comfortable and homely and full of character. There are log fires and plenty of books, but no television or smoking anywhere. Guests bring their own drinks and glasses are supplied. Evening meals may be booked by non-residents at 24 hours notice. The proprietors, Frank and Lesley Hart keep the Cross Keys homely and informal and make every effort to help you enjoy your stay. Guided walking and cooking holidays are also available.

The village of **Cautley** is on the A683 about three miles outside Sedbergh towards Kirkby Stephen, another stunning stretch of road to drive along, in the Rawthey Valley. The road follows the River Rauthey and is one of those beautiful routes through the high fells that few people find.

In Cautley, **St. Mark's** is a magnificent former vicarage built in 1872 for Cautley Church. Run by Barbara and Michael Wilson it is a two-fold

St. Mark's   Cautley   05396 20287

business, firstly offering excellent accommodation, with five very comfortable, en-suite rooms, and secondly, providing a variety of Creative
Leisure Courses throughout the year, which cover many disciplines, from
machine knitting to calligraphy. There are specialist instructors for all the
courses, ensuring expert tuition for both beginners and more experienced
students. In the evenings you can enjoy a home-cooked dinner in the
elegant dining room, then relax in front of a roaring fire in the study.

Devil's Bridge

Set in the shadow of the Howgills is **Cross Hall Farm Caravan and
Camping Park**, run by Thomas and Jennifer Harper and within a 100
acre working sheep and cattle farm. It is open from Easter to October

37

and provides a toilet block with washbasins and showers. There are four static six-berth caravans to let, with all the facilities you would expect, and room for a further five touring caravans, plus camping space available.

Cross Hall Farm   Cautley   05396 20668

For campers and walkers this is a perfect place to be based for a holiday, surrounded on all sides by the best English walking country, with the Lake District and the Yorkshire Dales National Parks to choose from.

CHAPTER TWO

The Upper Eden Valley

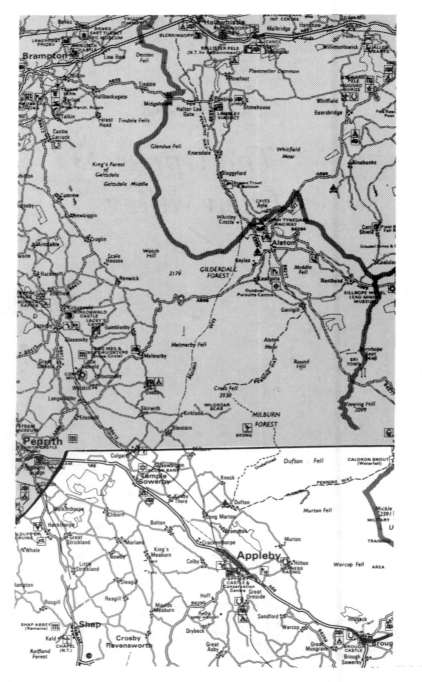

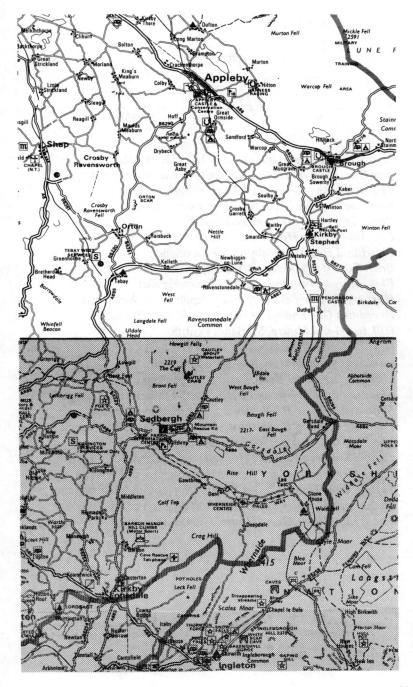

CHAPTER TWO

Index

Brougham Castle

The Upper Eden Valley

Crosby Garrett

CHAPTER TWO

The Upper
Eden Valley

The River Eden is entirely Cumbrian and one of the few large rivers in England that flows northwards. It rises on the edge of the Yorkshire Dales, in the fells above Mallerstang, and ends its journey in the Solway Firth. Carved through boulder clay and red sandstone and sandwiched between the Lakeland Fells and the Northern Pennines, the Eden Valley is green and fertile - in every sense another 'Eden'. But the valley was vulnerable to Scottish raids in medieval times and the number of pele towers and castles in the area are testament to a turbulent and often violent past.

The Eden shares its course with the famous Settle-Carlisle railway line, whose highest point is at Aisgill (1169 ft). Here it is joined by the infant river before descending through the steeply sided valley of Mallerstang. This is a particularly remote and beautiful area; to the west is Wild Boar Fell, a great brooding, flat-topped peak where reputedly the last wild boar in England was killed. Tucked down in the valley are the romantic ruins of Lammerside and Pendragon Castles. Lammerside originally dates from the 12th century but only the remains of the keep survive. **Pendragon Castle** is shrouded in legend which claims it to be the castle of Uther Pendragon, father of King Arthur, in the 6th century.Its name suggests that the castle was built by Uther, but at that time it would have been made of wood. It was some time after 1092 that William Rufus, having conquered Carlisle, built a stone pele tower at Pendragon to guard the pass of Mallerstang. In 1268 the castle passed into the hands of the Clifford family. Twice it was burned by the Scots and repaired by the family, the second time, in 1660, by the most famous member of that family, Lady Anne Clifford.

Between Garsdale Head and Kirkby Stephen, the B6259 follows the dramatic course of this valley, along with the Eden and the Settle-Carlisle railway line. Three miles from Garsdale Head, you will come to the remote hamlet of **Mallerstang**, where you should call in at **Aisgill Crafts**, an impressive building constructed alongside the railway in

1876, the year the line opened. Now a first-rate craft shop, tearoom and bed and breakfast establishment, Aisgill Crafts has been run since 1986 by Bill and Pauline Hasted. As well as housing a fascinating display of local crafts, the ground floor contains a tearoom where visitors can enjoy delicious teas, coffees, homemade cakes and savouries. Upstairs, there are three cosy guest rooms, and within the grounds, there are two well-appointed four-berth letting caravans. Aisgill Crafts is open all year.

Aisgill Crafts   Mallerstang   07683 72011

About a mile north of Pendragon Castle is the village of **Outhgill**. Here, truly outstanding country house accommodation is offered by Greta and Archie Naysmith at their superb home, **Cocklake House**, built between 1660 and 1670 by Lady Anne Clifford as a gatehouse to Pendragon Castle. Since moving to Cocklake House in 1987, Greta and Archie have carried out a series of tasteful improvements to their home. They now have two luxurious letting bedrooms available for guests, both beautifully decorated and equipped with their own large private bathrooms. Those fortunate enough to stay here are provided with superb accommodation and wonderful hospitality. As well as a fine English breakfast, guests have the option of having delicious evening meals which are prepared using fresh locally-sourced ingredients and are enjoyed in the relaxed informal atmosphere of the dining room. Most of the rooms in Cocklake House command breathtaking views of Pendragon Castle and the rocky fells above Mallerstang. This is an excellent base for exploring Mallerstang and for touring the Eden Valley, the Yorkshire Dales, the Lake District and beyond. For accurate directions, telephone the owners on 07683 72080 – it's certainly worth making the effort to find.

St Mary's Church in Outhgill, first built in 1311, was also repaired by Lady Anne. Indeed, from 1643, when she finally got possession of the

Clifford estates, 38 years after her father's death, until 1675 she devoted her life to restoring her properties and living in each of them for varying periods of time. The etates included six castles, Skipton and Barden in West Yorkshire and Appleby, Brough, Brougham and Pendragon in Westmorland. She even repaired the ancient Roman road between Wensleydale and the Eden Valley, the route she so often took to travel between her beloved Eden Valley castles and her birthplace, Skipton. Locals called it Lady Anne's Way. It is also aptly called the High Way, as it was 'worked' for many years by highwaymen, and none more notorious than Dick Turpin and William 'Swift Nick' Nevison.

Beyond Pendragon a narrow lane swings westward off the A683 Sedburgh to Kirkby Stephen Road, over the shoulder of Wild Boar Fell to **Ravenstonedale** (or Rissendale, as it is known locally), passing through some superb limetone scenery with great rock outcrops and the crumbling remains of once flourishing lime-kilns. Ravenstonedale lies on the very edge of the Howgill Fells and is a pretty, fellside village of stone-built cottages around Scandal Beck. The Parish Church of St Oswald is especially interesting. Built in 1738, it is one of the few Georgian churches in Cumbria. An earlier church had a separate bell-tower which rested on pillars and at its centre hung a refuge bell. Anyone guilty of a capital offence who managed to escape to Ravenstonedale and sound the bell was free from arrest by the King's officials. This custom was finally abolished in the reign of James I.

Cocklake House   Mallerstang   07683 72080

The present church, surrounded by yew trees, is particularly unusual with its bow pews facing one another and its three-decker pulpit complete with a sounding board and a seat for the parson's wife. The window at the east end commemorates the last woman in England to be put to death for her protestant faith. Elizabeth Gaunt was sentenced in 1638 by the

47

notorious Judge Jeffries to be burnt at the stake for sheltering a fugitive rebel.

At **Kirkby Stephen** the Eden Valley widens into a fertile plain of red sandstone villages, well tended farms and small market towns. Kirkby Stephen is old. It was the Norsemen who first established a village here and the Vikings named it, 'Kirke and bye', meaning churchtown. Although essentially part of the Eden Valley, Kirkby Stephen has a strong Yorkshire Dales feel about it. Indeed, the Church of St. Stephens, with its long, elegant nave, has been called "the cathedral of the Dales".

The church dates from 1220, with a 16th century tower, and is one of the finest churches in the Eastern fells, dominating the northern end of the town from its elevated position. Until the last century the Trupp Stone in the churchyard received money from local people every Easter Monday in payment of church tithes. At eight o'clock the curfew is still sounded by the Taggy Bell, once regarded by local children as a demon. Inside the church are a number of pre-Conquest stones, some of which show Norse influence. The most remarkable is the 8th century Loki stone, of which there are only two in Europe. Loki was a Norse God and presumably Viking settlers brought the belief in Loki to Kirkby Stephen. The carving of Loki shows a figure resembling the devil with sheep's horns, whose legs and arms are bound by heavy irons. This image is symbolic of the overpowering of Paganism by Christian beliefs. For many years the stone lay undiscovered, re-used as a building stone.

The tomb of Sir Richard De Musgrave of Harcla Castle is also in this church. He was the man reputed to have killed the last wild boar in England on what is now called Wild Boar Fell, and the story was given credence when some years ago the tomb was opened to reveal the bones of a man and woman alongside two tusks from a boar.

Between the church and the market-place stand the cloisters which served for a long time as a butter market. The market itself has existed since 1351 and has always been a focus for the surrounding countryside, whose industry was largely agricultural. In the 18th century knitting - mostly of stockings - was the most important manufacture of the town, and a restored spinning gallery reflects the importance of the woollen industry.

Two minutes walk from Kirkby Stephen's historic market square, on Silver Street, is the first-rate bed and breakfast establishment, **Redmayne House**. This attractive listed residence was built in the late 18th-century and extended in the 19th-century. Inside, it has a panelled Georgian dining room, an elegant Victorian drawing room and a number of tastefully decorated bedrooms which are extremely spacious and comfortable. (Look out for the original Victorian WC.) Owners Cathy and

Nick Prime provide their guests with a delicious English breakfast; they bake their own bread and use fresh locally-grown produce wherever possible. Residents are welcome to enjoy the large attractive garden at the rear. Redmayne House is open all year round except over the Christmas period but is unsuitable for smokers.

Redmayne House   Kirkby Stephen   07683 71441

If you are looking for a memento of Kirkby Stephen, **Heredities** on Hobsons lane is a veritable treasure trove. It was here in the 1950's that they first introduced the technological innovation of 'cold cast sculpture', a means of producing sculptures that in every way resembled poured bronze, but at a fraction of the cost. Famous for the wonderful range of over 80 different sculptures created by leading artists, Heredities has something to suit every taste and pocket. In addition to the many beautiful sculptures and figurines, there is also a range of imported quality giftware, including Toyo hand painted porcelain and Sandicast, a collection of stone cast animals.

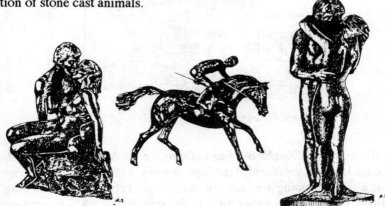

Heredities Ltd.   Kirkby Stephen   07683 71543

There are many delightful walks from Kirkby Stephen, for example to Croglam earthworks, a pre-historic fort, or to nearby Stenkrith Park. There are also some pleasant strolls along the riverside to a fine waterfall where the River Eden cascades into Coop Karnel Hole. Look out for the unusual shapes of the weathered limestone rock.

The village of **Nateby**, close to Kirkby Stephen, is well worth visiting. The road follows the old corpse-route over Coffin Bridge, along which the dead were taken to Kirkby Stephen to be buried. The village is now a quiet hamlet of houses standing alongside a beck. For centuries previously it was dominated by Hartley Castle, probably built in the 13th century and the home of Sir Andrew De Harcala, a great soldier during the reign of Edward II. Harcala was one of the first men to fight on a pony and he was made Earl of Carlisle in recognition of his service to the Crown. However, his failure to prevent Robert the Bruce invading the North of England led him to be accused of treason and he was executed in 1325. His castle was finally demolished by the Musgrave family who used the stone to build their Manor House at Edenhall.

Above Hartley you can still see the early bellpits in which copper and lead were mined and there is a fine walk from the village up to Nine Standards Rigg, one of the Eden Valley's most imposing landmarks. The cairns mark the old boundary between Yorkshire and Westmorland. According to legend they were first erected to represent the flags, or standards, of a great English army camped between the passes of Stainmore and Mallerstang.

Carmel Guest House   Tebay   05874 651

To the west of Kirkby Stephen is **Tebay**, on the A685 road to Kendal. The road follows the course of the upper reaches of the River Lune. At one time a sheep-farming area and railway village, Tebay, a long rambling village, now owes its importance to the arrival of the M6 motorway,

Cumbria's main thoroughfare.While this may not be a particularly attractive asset, its very central and easily accessible location makes this a very convenient base for touring Cumbria, and the surrounding scenery is just as beautiful.

On the southern edge of the village is **Carmel House**, a charming stone-built guesthouse which is owned and personally-run by Jack and Sue Marsden, two delightful hosts who for nine years ran the local pub. Their house contains seven well-appointed guest bedrooms (four doubles, two singles, one twin), all with en suite facilities, colour televisions and beverage making facilities, and is open all year round except during Christmas week (Note: the accommodation is unsuitable for pets).

Flakebridge Farmhouse   Tebay   05396 23661

Also close toTebay, and situated in 200 acres of magnificent Cumbrian countryside, **Flakebridge Farmhouse** is a working sheep and cattle farm run by Sandra and Norman Dodd. The house was built in 1787 and structurally has remained the same ever since. It is cosy and full of atmosphere, providing two tastefully decorated guest rooms with good facilities, and a comfortable guest lounge with TV. Visitors can expect a hearty farmhouse breakfast each morning and afterwards may well enjoy a fascinating chat with Norman, who devotes his time to breeding and exhibiting sheep, with much success if his trophy cabinet is anything to go by. Altogether a lovely, welcoming establishment.

About a mile to the north of Kirkby Stephen towards Brough, turn east off the A685 to reach the quiet and picturesque hamlet of **Winton**, which in old English, means "pasture farmland". It is built on a spring-line and like many other Cumbrian villages of medieval origin, once followed the *runrig*, or two-field system of agriculture. You can still find the evidence in long, thin fields to the north of the village. These would have been individual strips in medieval, open fields which were enclosed in the 17th

51

and 18th centuries. In the centre of the village is the manor house built in 1726, Winton's only three-storey building. It was formerly a boys' school where apparently the boys were treated like prisoners and not allowed to return home until the end of their education in case they told of their life at the school, The oldest building is Winton Hall, built of stone and dated 1665, but its appearance suggests it to be older with its stone buttresses and mullioned windows with iron bars.

In a splendid position overlooking Winton's village green is the **Bay Horse Inn**, an impressive pub, eating place and bed and breakfast establishment which is well worth making a detour to visit. Originally constructed between 1620 and 1630 as a farmhouse, the building became an alehouse late in the 17th-century and then an inn early in the 18th-century. At one time, part of the building was used to keep a horse and dray which belonged to a local Kirkby Stephen brewer.

Bay Horse Inn   Winton   07683 71451

The present-day inn still retains much of its original character and charm with attractive white-painted walls and a cosy traditional interior. It has been owned and personally run since 1985 by Sheila and Derek Parvin, two fine hosts who have been successful in creating a truly relaxed and welcoming atmosphere. The inn is a free house and during the summer months, stocks as many as five traditional hand-pulled ales, all well kept and served in top-class condition. An extensive menu of delicious bar meals is also served every lunchtime and evening. All dishes are homemade and come in generous portions at surprisingly reasonable prices. Sheila and Derek have also created three tastefully decorated letting bedrooms which are available all year round. These all have central heating, en suite facilities and are appointed to a good modern standard. In fine weather, customers are welcome to sit out in the attractive garden which is situated to the rear of the inn. All in all, the Bay

Kirkby Stephen

Horse Inn offers excellent food, drink and hospitality.

Walking on Winton Fell you are more than likely to see red grouse lifting off from the large tracts of heather on the fellside. Indeed the wildlife is much more prolific around this area where the limestone provides more plentiful food than on the fells around the lakes.

A few miles from **Winton** is **Kaber** which, in 1663, was the scene of the Kaber Rigg plot, a rebellion against Charles II. It was led by Captain Robert Atkinson of Watergate Farm in Mallerstang. The rising failed and Atkinson was hung, drawn and quartered at Appleby; tragically, a messenger carrying his reprieve was delayed on Stainmore.

The small town of **Brough**, which stands at the point where the Stainmore Pass opens into the Vale of Eden, is, in effect,two settlements - Church Brough and Market Brough. Church Brough is a group of neat houses and cottages clustered around a little market square in which a maypole stands on the site of a former market-cross. Brough Castle is built within the ramparts of the Roman camp of Verterae, constructed to protect the Roman road over Stainmore Pass. The building of the Norman castle was begun by William Rufus in 1095 but it was largely destroyed in 1174 by William the Lion of Scotland. Many times Scottish raiders laid seige to Brough Castle and fierce battles were fought. An ancient ballad tells of the legendary bravery of one knight from Brough who defended the tower alone after his comrades had fallen. He was finally vanquished when the Scottish army set fire to the tower, but the incident was so dramatic that it went into the realms of storytelling and was remembered in the ballad of the Valiant Knight of Brough. This was another castle that was restored by the remarkable Lady Anne Clifford in 1650. The castle, with its tall keep, is now under the ownership of English Heritage and is well worth visiting, if only for the superb panorama of the surrounding fells to be seen from the battlements.

Market Brough is also an ancient settlement and was particularly important in the 18th and 19th centuries when it became a major coaching-town on stage-coach routes between England and Scotland. It was on the junction of several routes and boasted more than ten inns. However, the width and breadth of its High Street also indicates its importance as a market town. It was granted a charter in 1330 enabling it to hold a weekly market as well as four cattle markets and an annual fair.

One custom still celebrated in Brough is the Twelfth Night Holly-Burning, a unique festival with pagan origins. Spend some time exploring Brough; look for the beautiful 17th century carved lintel of the Grapes Inn and a delightful, hidden pack-horse bridge near Mill House.

To the east of Brough, Stainmore Pass carries the A66 through a remote area of the North Pennines described by David Bellamy as

'England's last wilderness'. Here you will find the historic **Punch Bowl**, an 18th-century former coaching inn which is owned and personally-run by Stuart and Constance Davey. The inn is said to have been one of Dick Turpin's hideouts and there is reputedly a 250-yard escape tunnel connected to the basement. One of the staff passageways is even said to be haunted by the ghost of a man murdered following an argument over stolen booty. Today, Stuart and Constance provide more conventional hospitality. They serve a first-rate pint, excellent home-cooked meals and have five comfortable letting rooms available all year round.

The Punch Bowl   North Stainmore   07683 41262

Near Stainnmore Summit are the foundations of Maiden Castle, a Roman fort built to guard the pass against marauders. A few yards over the Cumbrian border, into County Durham, is the stump of the ancient Rey Cross which was erected before AD946 and which, until 1092, marked the boudary between England and Scotland. It is thought to be the site of the battle at which the last Viking King of York and Northern England, Eric Bloodaxe, was killed following his expulsion from the city.

The distinctive, low hills that lie between Brough and **Musgrave** are drumlins - heaps of material deposited by the glaciers. In this area many drumlins are marked by broad, grassy ridges, remains of ancient lynchets or ploughing strips. There are some particularly interesting and relatively little known villages along this stretch of the Eden, such as **Soulby**, which stands on the wide, grassy banks of Scandal Beck.

Soulby is about three miles outside Kirkby Stephen, and here you will find **Bonnygate Farm**. This is a 300 acre working beef and dairy farm which has been in the Bainbridge family for over 50 years. Mrs. Bainbridge has been providing a bed and breakfast service for the past 18 years and visitors here are assured of a warm welcome and a comfortable stay in three spacious guest rooms. As well as a full farmhouse breakfast, there is an optional evening meal provided, whilst for those who prefer, there is also a self-catering cottage available.

Bonnygate Farm   Soulby   07683 71347

Another such village is nearby **Crosby Garrett**, dominated by the viaducts of the Settle - Carlisle railway. Local legend has it that the Devil, seeing all the stones lying ready to build Crosby Garrett Church, carried them in his leather apron to the top of a nearby hill. He reasoned that, as people grew old, they would be unable to climb the hill and attend church and thus would come to him rather than go to Heaven. Such tales apart, the church itself is said to be of Anglo-saxon origin though the visible fabric is 12th century. Inside there are some superb carvings, particularly near the font. The church is also famous for its tunnel, or hagioscope, cut through the wall to allow people in the north aisle to see the altar. Near the church gates is a tithe barn, built in the 18th century to store farm produce and given to the church as a religious tax.

Eden Gate   Warcop   07683 41242

Warcop, just off the A66 Brough to Appleby road, grew up as a crossing point on the Eden. It lies at the foot of one of the oldest bridges to cross the river, dating from the 16th century and red sandstone buildings surround the village green with its maypole in the centre. On the hills above the village are stones, cairns and the remains of what is claimed to be a druid's temple. The church of St Columba is built outside the village on the site of a Roman camp. An interesting building in its own right, it is particularly famous for its rush-bearing ceremony which takes place in June each year. Close by is **Dyke Nook Farm Museum**, with a fine collection of heavy horses and farm animals.

In Warcop you will find **Eden Gate**, a magnificent Georgian house owned by Pat and Harry]ones who provide first class bed and breakfast accommodation. Reached by a long, sweeping drive, the house stands in four acres of attractive gardens and was built in 1820. Eden Gate is a homely relaxing place to stay, providing four outstanding letting rooms, attractively decorated and with all the modern facilities you would expect. Breakfast in the newly completed conservatory gives a relaxing start to your day before setting out to explore the surrounding area of this tranquil corner of Cumbria.

Haybergill House   Warcop   07683 41464

Near Warcop top quality country house bed and breakfast accommodation is provided by Keith and Maureen Balmer at their impressive Edwardian home, **Haybergill House**. Set in two-and-a-half acres of lovely wooded grounds, the house stands within a quarter-of-a-mile of the A66. It was built in 1911 as a shooting lodge for General Sir Arthur Singleton-Wynne and contains some wonderful hidden treasures: there is a wardrobe from Lowther Castle, panelling made from ships' timbers and a magnificent staircase and two mahogany doors which were brought from the Tower of London. As well as offering three delightful letting bedrooms, Keith and Maureen have two six-berth static caravans available in the grounds.

Further down the river is **Great Ormside**, once an important fort guarded by a pele tower. The ancient church of St. James, which dates from the 11th century, occupies a site on a deep-sided defence mound. Relics of pre-Christian burials have been found in the mound, as well as a Viking sword (now in the Tullie Museum in Carlisle). A silver-gilt and enamel bowl from the 7th century has also been found. It is regarded as one of the most important pieces of Anglo-saxon metalware to survive and is a particularly beautiful piece, richly decorated with vine-scrolls, birds and animals. The bowl is now on permanent display in the Yorkshire Museum in York.

A field path leads to **Little Ormside** with its large Cedar Tree said to have been brought back from Lebanon as a sapling by General Whitehead. On the voyage home he grew it in his hat and shared his daily ration of one pint of water with it.

Above Ormside, and just north of Grange Scar, is the pretty village of **Great Asby**, set in a wooded hollow, through which Hoff Beck runs. Beside the stream is St. Helen's Well, walled on three sides and siad never to run dry or freeze. Nearby are the splendid alms-houses of St. Helen's, built between 1811 and 1820, and across the footbridge is Asby Hall. The Hall once belonged to the Musgrave family of Edenhall and you can still see their crest and coat-of-arms above the door. An added bonus for visitors is the delightful village pub and eating place, the **Three Grey-hounds Inn**, which dates from the early 1700s. Inside, it has a wonderful traditional atmosphere with open log fires and an interesting collection of historic memorabilia on the walls. Margaret and John Hughes have built up an excellent reputation for providing the very best in food, drink and hospitality. As well as a selection of well-kept traditional ales, they serve an extensive range of good value meals including childrens and vegetarian menus (Tel: 07683 51428).

Appleby-in-Westmorland is the old county town of Westmorland, and one of the most delightful small towns in England. It was built by the Norman Ranulph de Meschines, in a defensive curve, protected on three sides by the loop of the River Eden and on the fourth by Castle Hill. By the middle of the 12th century the church of St. Lawrence had been founded, a market established and burgage plots laid out behind the cottages which lined the main street. It continued to rise in importance, but in 1388 was almost completely destroyed by Scottish raiders, and then devastated by plague in 1598.

St. Lawrence Church now dates mainly from the 14th century and much of it was restored by Lady Anne Clifford in the 17th century. In the Clifford Chapel are the beautiful alabaster effigy of Lady Anne's mother Margaret, Countess of Cumberland, and the monument to Lady Anne

Orton

herself, with a lavish display of heraldry, one of her great loves. The organ, which was brought from Carlisle Cathedral in 1684, is the oldest working organ in Britain.

Tufton Arms Hotel   Appleby-in-Westmorland   07683 51593

The main street, Boroughgate, with the church at the bottom end of it, has the black and white Moot Hall of 1596 on an island site in the middle of the wide street. In the market square, **The Tufton Arms** is an impressive Victorian coaching inn. Despite its size, it is very much a family business with every member of the Milsom family contributing to the smooth running of this magnificent establishment. There are 19 bedrooms ranging from luxury suites to single rooms, providing accommodation for everyone, whatever your needs. All are beautifully decorated and carefully furnished to retain the hotel's Victorian feel, yet at the same time equipped with every modern facility for 20th century comfort. On the ground floor you can relax in the comfortable oak panelled Victorian bar, before making your way to the Conservatory Restaurant. Here, the atmosphere is reminiscent of the Raj, with cane furniture and an exotic backdrop of brightly coloured birds and foliage. You will be spoilt for choice by the excellent gourmet and table d'hote menus created by David Milsom. The emphasis is always on fresh local produce imaginatively prepared, and the extensive menu includes a first class range of fish dishes. It seems appropriate therefore that The Tufton Arms offers excellent four day fishing courses which provide expert tuition for all abilities. Each day starts with tuition and practice followed by practical experience on the riverbank going on until dusk if necessary, then back to the luxury and comfort of the hotel. The hotel also offers a 'Settle and Carlisle Steam Superbreak' which inlcudes two nights, dinner, bed and breakfast, a trip on the famous railway, and a guided coach tour of the outstanding Settle and Carlisle countryside. Other activities such as pony trekking and shooting are all readily available, so whatever you leisure pursuits, you will be well catered for at the Tufton Arms Hotel.

Each year, during the first week of June, Appleby Horse Fair takes place with gypsies and dealers arriving in elegant, decorative motor and horse-drawn caravans. The trade, principally in horses, is a picturesque and colourful spectacle and the origins of the fair date to a charter granted in 1685 by James II.

A few yards off the main street in an area called High Wiend, you will find **The Black Boy** licensed restaurant. This charming establishment was originally built in 1677 and named after Charles II who was known as the Black Boy because of his long dark curls. Through the listed front door you will find two cosy beamed dining areas. In one there is a feature stone fireplace and in the other a very old locally made kitchen range. Both rooms are beautifully decorated, as is the comfortable bar area upstairs, where you can relax with an aperitif before sampling the excellent value mouthwatering dishes available. A popular eating house, The Black Boy is a place not to be missed.

The Black Boy   Appleby- in-Westmorland   07683 52368

The upper part of Boroughgate is lined with fine Georgian houses set back from the road. On the left there is an archway and porch with a hanging bell. Through the archway in the seclusion of a cobbled court-yard is St Anne's Hospital, almshouses founded by Lady Anne Clifford for elderly women.

Appleby Castle, at the top of Boroughgate and overlooking the town, is as ancient as any in the Eden Valley but is one of the best preserved. It, too, was restored by Lady Anne, and her ghost is said to wander the castle, although many say she was too good to have a ghost and her soul must be in heaven. Beyond the Lodge Gates the massive Norman Keep dominates the castle, built between 1110 and 1120. The Great Hall is of special interest as it contains several paintings of the Clifford family, the most important of which is entitled simply, "The Great Picture". The castle grounds are now a Rare Breeds Survival Centre which shelters endangered species of domestic and wild animals and birds. The Keep and the grounds are open to the public in the summer months.

Bongate, on the other side of the river, is the older part of Appleby, founded by the Vikings over a thousand years ago.

Courtfield Hotel   Appleby-in-Westmorland   07683 51394

On the edge of Appleby you will find the **Courtfield Hotel**. This former vicarage was built during the 19th century and has been owned and run by Alan and Alice Robinson for the past 28 years. These fine hosts offer a warm welcome to all their guests and provide excellent accommodation in eleven tastefully decorated letting rooms, some en-suite and all with colour TV and hot drinks facilities. There is a cosy and friendly guest lounge as well as a separate bar area, and in the pleasantly intimate dining room the Robinsons specialise in providing a varied menu of wholesome home-cooked food. To accompany your meal you can choose from the extensive wine list which includes over twenty different wines.

Delightful farmhouse accommodation is offered by Mrs Yvonne Dent at **Meadow Ing Farm**, a 105-acre working dairy farm specialising in pedigree Holstein cattle which is situated just off the A66 at **Crackenthorpe**, two miles northwest of Appleby. The farmhouse was constructed to a traditional design in 1984 of local stone taken from a nearby barn. Inside, it is appointed to a very high standard with full central heating and antique furniture. There is a separate guests' lounge with an open fire and colour television, a traditionally decorated dining area and two comfortable letting bedrooms containing examples of Yvonne's patchwork-making skills. Evening meals are available by arrangement. The accommodation is available all year round except at Christmas but is unsuitable for smokers.

Meadow Ing Farm   Crackenthorpe   07683 52543

To the north of Appleby are the three settlements of **Murton**, **Dufton** and **Knock** with their distinctive conical hills close by, each named after its village and all with superb viewpoints.

Dufton is a delightful, tiny hamlet , signposted off the main Appleby-Penrith road. It is well worth stopping off here to visit **The Stag Inn**. Overlooking the village green, this lovely old-fashioned village pub has been owned and personally run by Helen and Cecil Coxon since April 1992. A freehouse, it is a cosy and welcoming establishment where you can warm yourself by the log fire on cold evenings, or refresh yourself with a cool drink outside on warm summer days. Open all day from 8.00am, The Stag provides excellent, very reasonably priced meals throughout the day and with its terrific village pub atmosphere, is a place not to be missed.

Behind the village of Dufton lies Dufton Gill, a beautiful, secret, wooded valley through which runs a footpath. From Dufton there is a track carrying The Pennine Way that leads up to High Cup Nick, a great horse-shoe precipice at the edge of the Northern Pennine escarpment formed by a glacial lake during the Ice Age.

In the shadow of the Great Dunn Fell is Milburn, built for defence against the Scots. All the houses of the village face inwards onto a rectangular green, presenting four solid walls to the outside world. The narrow entrances at the four corners were sealed each winter until 1826, leaving only narrow 'through-gangs', which could be easily blocked under attack.

The Stag Inn   Gullom   07683 61401

Not to be confused with its namesake in Dufton, **The Stag Inn** at **Gullom**, near Milburn, may not be easy to find, since Gullom is not listed on many maps. Barely a hamlet, the total population of this tiny place is fourteen, but the presence of the inn makes a trip here a must. This 17th century inn is run by Alan and Thelma Knell who over the past four years have injected a life and enthusiasm into this establishment without detracting at all from its charming original character. Open all day, The Stag provides first class ales and excellent food. The attached barn is a fabulous dining and entertainment area providing live entertainment every weekend when they have an extended license. Alan lays on a minibus so that you can forget about driving home, although if available, the two self-catering cottages in the recently converted barn make an ideal place to stay.

Returning towards the main A66 from Milburn you pass the pretty village of **Newbiggin**, at the confluence of Milburn and Crowdundle Becks, and then **Kirkby Thore**. About one and a half miles out of the village of Kirkby Thore, you will see a sign for **Low Abbey Cottages**, a

Low Abbey Cottages   Kirkby Thore   07683 61207

group of four traditional cottages offering first class self-catering accommodation. Enjoying a quiet, safe location on a private access drive, the cottages are on a ridge above the owners' working farm and offer fabulous views of the surrounding countryside. Large parties of up to 24 can be catered for, with all four cottages sleeping between six and seven and providing excellent facilities including colour TV, microwave, barbecue and garden furniture, logs for the open fire, a shared laundry room, plus free use of a cot and highchair if required. A big attraction for the whole family is the heated indoor swimming pool which is housed within a converted barn and provides hours of fun whatever the weather. The farm itself is another major attraction with its variety of animals, some of which are newer continental breeds. On fine days you can have a your lunch at the picnic table opposite the cottages, whilst the children make the most of the marvellous childrens' play area alongside. On weekend evenings you can make use of the mini bus service to the local pub a mile away, which provides good bar meals and has a late night licence, so you can stay and enjoy the evening's entertainment without having to worry about driving. Low Abbey Cottages make an ideal touring base.

A little further along the A66, about four miles from Penrith is **Temple Sowerby**, a picturesque village with red sandstone buildings around a green, and once the home of the Order of Knights Templar who ruled the community until 1312. A walk through the delightful Oak Wood takes you to Acorn Bank, an 18th century Manor House, now a National Trust property whose herb garden, with its magnificent display of both culinary and medicinal herbs, is open to the public.

This pretty Cumbrian village is the location for **The Temple Sowerby Country House Hotel**, an impressive and elegant establishment run by resident owners, Anne and Peter McNamara. An old Cumbrian farm-house with Georgian additions it stands in two acres of well tended gardens and overlooks Cross Fell, the highest peak in the Pennines, renowned for its spectacular ridge walk. Decorated in a style that enhances its age and character, the hotel is full of lovely antique furniture, carefully chosen pictures and prints, and pretty ornaments. The down-stairs drawing room is warm and inviting and the perfect place to relax, with comfortable chairs and an open log fire for those chilly winter evenings. In Spring and Summer, guests often choose to enjoy a drink in the conservatory or on the terrace which overlooks the magnificent walled garden. There is also a small cocktail lounge where during the day you can enjoy morning coffee, light lunches and afternoon teas. The talented chef, Pauline Wilson makes the homemade preserves, cakes and biscuits, as well as the mouthwatering five course dinner which is served each evening in the elegant and intimate dining room with its panelled walls and exposed beams. At the end of the day you can retire to one of the twelve excellently equipped bedrooms, two with four posters and all with en-suite bathroom. Four of the bedrooms are situated a few yards away from the main house in the converted Coach House, and two of these are on the ground floor and are suitable for the disabled. Whether as a stopping off point on a journey, or an escape from the stresses of everyday life, Temple Sowerby Country House Hotel is the perfect retreat.

Temple Sowerby Guest House Temple Sowerby 07683 61578

Just south of Temple Sowerby is **Cliburn**, where there are magnifi-cent views from the Church of St Cuthbert, which possesses one of the earliest Jerusalem crosses in existence. It originally came from Vallom-brosa Monastery in Italy where it had been for 700 years. The Cross is made from Gethsemane olive and ivory, inlain with pearl and gold. It was given to the church by Admiral Cliburn, who is also remembered in the font cover.

South of Cliburn is the picturesque village of **Morland**. The tranquility of this area belies the fact that the motorway is only a few minutes drive away, but here in this quiet unspoilt corner, you will find **Hill Top Guest House**. This lovely Georgian house provides first class accommodation in the form of three en-suite guest rooms, all with excellent facilities. Downstairs the welcoming atmosphere of the cosy lounge with its feature fireplace ensures total relaxation. All the windows at Hill Top enjoy superb views of the surrounding countryside and should you wish, activities such as walking, pony trekking, fishing, or even playing golf are easily accessible from here. Further south, following the River Lyvennet from Morland, you will meet up with the river at two tiny, unspoilt villages, Mauld's Meaburn and just beyond, **Crosby Ravensworth**.

Hill Top Guest House   Morland   0931 714561

The road from Crosby Ravensworth to **Orton** is one of the loveliest in East Cumbria, passing superb limestone scenery. The village itself stands below Orton Scar. Orton was the birthplace of George Whitehead (1636-1723) who, with George Fox, was one of the founders of the early Quaker movement. The church, in common with many in the Eden Valley, has a massive 16th century tower built for defence - a necessary precaution. On Orton Scar a beacon was lit to warn people to tend their flocks and herds and seek safety from the feared Scottish raiders.

Back on the A66, two miles east of Penrith, turn north off the A66 Brough road at **Brougham** and find historic **Hornby Hall**. Now a magnificent country guesthouse, this impressive manor farmhouse was constructed of local red sandstone about 1550 by Edward Birkbeck on a site which was formerly owned by the Cliffords, one of the four great baronial families of the northern borderlands. (It is said that John, the ninth Lord Clifford (c1435-1461), was responsible for the cold-blooded murder of the Earl of Rutland, an event which was described by Shakespeare in *King Henry VI Part III*.)

Now Grade II listed, the present-day Hornby Hall stands on a working farm surrounded by beautiful tranquil countryside. Since the end of World War II, it has been in the hands of the Pollock family who in 1991, carried out a major refurbishment to convert it into a superb country guesthouse. The 16th-century Hall is now used as a dining room and has an original sandstone-flagged floor, huge refectory tables and a large open fireplace containing a Victorian range. There is also a delightful guests' sitting room and a number of comfortable bedrooms, all of which face south. The two double rooms have en suite facilities and the three twin rooms share a bathroom and shower room. Two further bedrooms have recently been opened in the ancient tower.

Hornby Hall   Brougham   0768 89114

As well as delicious English breakfasts, traditional three-course meals are served each evening. These are prepared according to old-fashioned country recipes using fresh locally-grown produce. Hornby Hall also possesses a residential licence and offers a good range of wines and beers. Dry fly trout fishing is available on a nearby stretch of the River Eamont for which day tickets can be purchased (open season 15 March to 30 September). Alternatively, there are also some marvellous walks for those preferring to explore the surrounding area on foot.

Approaching Penrith from the south, on the A6, you will pass through the village of **Clifton. The White House** is a lovely country guest house for non-smokers, run by Anne and Christine Broadbent. Ideally situated as a base for touring the Lakes, the Eden Valley and local places of interest, this magnificent house stands proudly overlooking open countryside with views towards Shap. Guests receive a warm welcome from

The White House   Clifton   0768 65115

these two sisters who have run The White House for the past five years. The accommodation is excellent and each homely guest room has its own individual character. Two of them rooms are en-suite and there are two further guest bathrooms. A four course evening meal is provided, offering lovely home-cooked food and excellent value.

Nearby, **The Wetheriggs Country Pottery and Museum** at Clifton Dyke is the country's only working museum dedicated to the history and traditions of the English Country Potteries. Indeed in 1973 The Department of the Environment declared the whole Wetheriggs site a national monument. Here you can watch traditional earthenwares being handmade or even have a go at creating one yourself. There are displays of 19th century industrial relics, and a huge collection of 18th and 19th century slipware pottery. The original beehive kiln is an impressive sight, and in the marvellous well stocked gift shop you can watch a video all about this amazing establishment. If lunchtime beckons, there is a

Wetheriggs Country Pottery   Clifton Dyke   0768 62946

licensed restaurant and a coffee shop, whilst for the children there is a well equipped play area.

From here it is only a few miles drive to the historic town of Penrith and on your way it is worth paying a visit to Dunmallott Hill Fort near Clifton for its beautiful views of Ullswater.

CHAPTER THREE

The Lower Eden Valley

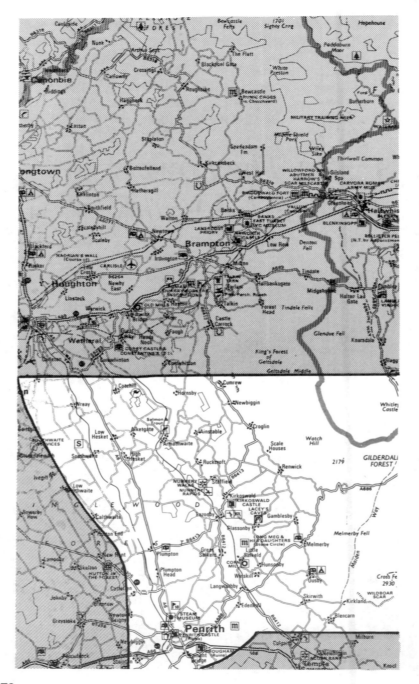

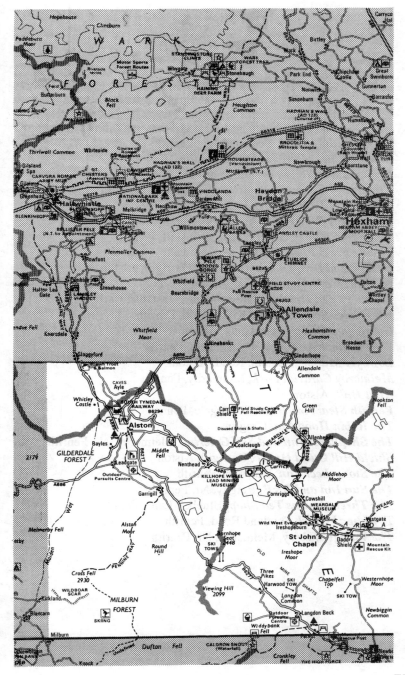

73

CHAPTER THREE

Index

'Long Meg', Little Salkeld

The Lower Eden Valley

CHAPTER THREE

The Lower Eden Valley

The red sandstone town of **Penrith** is dominated by Beacon Hill Pike, which stands amidst wooded slopes high above the town. The tower was built in 1719 and marks the place where, since 1296, beacons have been lighted to warn of war and invasion.The beacon was last lit during the Napoleonic wars in 1804. It was seen by the author Sir Walter Scott who was visiting Cumberland and it prompted him to hasten home to rejoin his local volunteer regiment. It is well worth the climb from Beacon's Edge, along the footpath to the summit, to enjoy a magnificent view of the Lakeland fells.

Penrith itself is a lively market town with handsome old buildings. It is a charming mixture of narrow streets and wide-open spaces, such as Great Dockray and Sandgate, into which cattle were once herded during the border raids. Later they became market places and markets are still held every Tuesday and Saturday.

Penrith has a splendid Georgian church in a very attractive church-yard, surrounded by a number of interesting buildings. The oldest part of St. Andrew's dates from Norman times but the most recent part, the nave, was rebuilt between 1719 and 1772. Of particular interest is the three-sided gallery. Look out for the brass candelabra, suspended from the roof, which was a gift from the Duke of Cumberland in 1745 - a reward for the town's loyalty during the Jacobite Rising.

Enjoying a peaceful location by the churchyard, the **Eden Craft Gallery** is the perfect place to pick up a special gift or holiday memento. This delightful establishment is run by the Eden Craft Association, a group of almost 40 craftspeople which was set up in 1982 and whose aim is to bring quality, handmade local products to the public at attractive prices. Through sheer hard work and determination, the Eden Craft Gallery is now a successful, well-established business which has a variety of crafts with something to appeal to everyone. Upstairs the cosy coffee shop is a lovely place to relax and admire the artwork adorning the walls, where you can sample the tasty, homecooked "crafts"!

Eden Craft Gallery   Penrith   0768 67955

Still in the churchyard, **Chataways Bistro** is owned and personally run by Jeff and Sarah Brades. The building was constructed in 1709 for a wealthy property owner and in its time has been a ropemaker's workshop and the home of a legendary local hermit. Inside, the atmosphere is relaxed and stylish with old beamed ceilings and elegantly prepared tables. While Jeff looks after the front-of-house activities, Sarah takes care of the cooking. Her menu changes monthly and features such appetising main courses as Cheshire lamb crumble, halibut Catalan, Dorset jugged beef and a choice of vegetarian dishes. You should book at weekends, as this is a popular place.

In the 9th and 10th centuries Penrith was the capital of Cumbria, a semi-independent state which, until AD1070, formed part of the Kingdom of Strathclyde and Scotland. It is said that the King of Cumbria, Owen Caesarius, is buried in the churchyard amidst the group of gravestones known as Giant's Grave. The group consists of two ancient crosses, each 11ft high, and four 10th-century "hogback" tombstones which have arched tops and sharply sloping sides.

Chataways Bistro   Penrith   0768 890233

The ruins of Penrith Castle bear witness to the town's important role in defending the surrounding country from marauding Scots. The castle was built around 1399, but was enlarged for the Duke of Gloucester (later Richard III) when he was Lord Warden of the Western Marches and responsible for keeping the peace along the border with Scotland. The castle has been in ruins since 1550 but remains an impressive monument.

You don't have to be a steam engine fanatic to appreciate the Penrith Steam Museum. Situated only a few hundred yards from the castle, on Castlegate, this amazing museum houses a magnificent collection of exhibits dating back to the early part of this century. From the main building where you can see traction engines, a fire engine, a brewery lorry and many more items, you enter the Blacksmith's Shop and Machine Room where you can watch craftsmen at work, often using very old tools and methods. Across the courtyard you can view a furnished Victorian cottage and alongside there is a further display with all kinds of items ranging from old motor cycles to bygone farming machinery. This is a place not to be missed, whatever your age.

Penrith Steam Museum   Penrith   0768 62154

While you are on Castlegate visit **Jane Pollock Antiques**. Housed in a late 19th century building, this shop is a haven for antique lovers and inquisitive browsers alike. Jane, the proprietor, has been here for ten years and has developed an extensive collection of 18th, 19th and 20th century items. Her main theme is silver and she has a beautiful display of canteens of cutlery of various styles and designs, as well as other magnificent pieces of silver. There is something here for everyone in a collection that will bring back fond memories for the older customers or arouse curiosity and interest in the young.

Jane Pollock Antiques   Penrith   0768 67211

If you are spending more than a couple of hours in Penrith, follow the Penrith Town Trail which passes some of the town's historic buildings. The Town Hall was originally two houses, designed by Robert Adam and built in 1791. Near the church is an impressive Tudor House which is now a restaurant but was, at one time, Dame Birkett's school attended by William Wordsworth, his sister Dorothy, and his future wife, Mary Hutchinson. The Town Trail leaflet is available at the Tourist Information Centre on Middlegate, and the trail begins from here, opposite Musgrave Hall, which is now occupied by the British Legion but was once the home of the Musgrave family of Edenhall, and their heraldic arms are still on a lintel aboe the doorway.

The first building of note on the Trail is the Town Hall, which was the result of modernisation of two former Adam style houses, one of which was known as Wordsworth House as it was the home of the poet's cousin, Captain John Wordsworth.

In Portland Place, just behind the Town Hall, visitors to Penrith will find excellent accommodation and friendly service when they visit **Brandelhow Guest House**. This elegant Victorian town house is owned by Carole Tully, who has twenty years experience of providing bed and breakfast and knows how to look after her guests. Throughout the house the decoration and furnishings are first class, with additional features of an original slate fire surround, beautiful alcoves and a magnificent staircase. With five spacious and well equipped guest rooms, a family can take up a double and three singles in the large family room and still there seems to be plenty of space to relax.

Brandelhow Guest House   Penrith   0768 64470

Just around the corner, for a first class traditional teashop, it would be hard to beat **The Three Crowns Teashop**. Just off Brunswick Road in Blue Bell Lane, it is housed in what were formerly two mid-18th century cottages and the range from one of the cottages is on view inside. Open from 9am to 5pm Monday to Saturday (Sundays in high season) this is the place to come when you need a little sustenance to continue exploring. The menu ranges from mouthwatering homemade cakes and scones, to freshly prepared sandwiches, or for those with a larger gap to fill, there are daily specials available. Excellent service combined with a warm, welcoming atmosphere and quality food, make The Three Crowns Teashop a rare treat indeed.

The Three Crowns Teashop   Penrith   0768 899789

The largest of Penrith's market spaces is known as Great Dockray. On its west side is the Gloucester Arms, formerly Dockray Hall. It is said that the Duke of Gloucester resided here, and his coat of arms appears above the main entrance. Apparently, a secret underground passage links the Gloucester Arms with the castle.

Townhead Hotel   Penrith   0768 62791

The Townhead Hotel is on Scotland Road, which is the main A6 heading out of Penrith town centre in the direction of Carlisle. It has nine guest bedrooms, all en-suite and all having colour television and tea and coffee making facilities. The hotel is licensed and is open to non-residents. The cosy, well-decorated restaurant will seat up to sixty diners with steaks and grills a speciality of the house. Sympathetically refurbished, the lounge retains its original beams and stone seats and, with its brasses and pictures, has an antique feel. The bar is very cosy and the warmth and friendliness of the owners, Len and Dawn Wilson is very much in evidence. Believed to be a 17th century half-way house for travellers between England and Scotland, the hotel is open all year round and children and pets are welcomed; there is ample car parking space.

Beacon Bank Hotel   Penrith   0768 62633

At Beacon Edge, on the outskirts of Penrith, overlooking the town stands an impressive Victorian country house, Beacon Bank Hotel. This

82

charming establishment provides a perfect touring base, being not only close to the town, but also within easy reach of the Lake District, the Borders, Southern Scotland and the beautiful Eden Valley. Owned and run by Barbara and Terry Black, Beacon Bank provides first class accommodation in six well decorated, en-suite guest rooms. Here the bed is the main feature and you will find four posters, half testers and even a carved French antique bed, giving an added taste of luxury. With additional options of a packed lunch and evening meal, Barbara and Terry aim to provide you with every comfort and apparently succeed.

Situated on the western bluff of the B6262, about 1 mile south of Penrith, is the magnificent **Brougham Hall**. Once nicknamed 'the Windsor of the North', this is an impressive Cumbrian mansion dating back to medieval times and currently undergoing extensive restoration. In its heyday, it was one of the North West's most spectacular buildings, with 39 bedrooms, a 12,000 book library, a fabulous collection of antique furniture and a Norman corridor painted with a copy of the Bayeux Tapestry.

The Hall and estate were bought by John Brougham, in 1726, and stayed in the Brougham family for several generations, during which time it was subject to restoration, extension and finally dereliction. Unfortunately in 1934 it was sold to Major Carleton-Cowper who, having never liked the Broughams, sold all the fixtures and fittings and then ordered the Hall's demolition. Parts of the outer walls and much of the Mansion House were destroyed before the Royal Armoured Corps took over the site in 1942, for the secret development of a tank with a 13 million candle power beam, intended to blind the enemy temporarily.

Brougham Hall   Penrith   0768 68184

The Hall and estate is now owned by Christopher Terry whose inspirational plans mean it is, at last, being restored to its former glory. The restored buildings are being converted into a variety of workshops and museums, including a Children's Educational Lakeland Museum in the Tudor Hall, and in the 17th century guard house, a shop selling ceramics based on 19th century designs, and a museum commemorating the 1745 Battle of Clifton Moor, which was fought in the meadows beneath the Hall.

Brougham Hall is open all year and visitors are welcome to visit the various workshops which are already on site. These include Rona Newsom's Smoke House, which supplies local outlets with smoked game, meat, cheeses and fish, also a hand made chocolate factory, goldsmith, jeweller, art metalworker, cabinet-maker, woodturner and stonemason, David Fawcett who works in local sandstone and slate. All sell their goods on site, so you can watch them at work and purchase a memento of your visit.

Nearby Brougham Castle, in a most picturesque setting on the banks of the River Eamont, is where Lady Anne Clifford died in 1676. This was another of her restoration projects; in earlier times the castle had been one of the most formidable in the Eden Valley, and defended the road across the Pennines from York to Carlisle. The castle is now preserved by English Heritage, and is one of relatively few that is open all year (but not on Mondays in winter). It also houses an interesting, small exhibition of Roman tombstones from the nearby fort.

Sun Inn   Newton Reigny   0768 67055

Two miles northwest of Penrith, the minor country roads lead to **Newton Reigny**, an attractive hamlet which can be found midway between Junctions 40 and 41 to the west of the M6. Here, you will find the historic **Sun Inn**, an impressive free house which is run by David and Sue Hair and Barry and Shirley Pickles. Since taking over in 1991, they have been successful in creating an atmosphere which is both stylish and welcoming. They serve an excellent menu of home-cooked dishes which offers goodies like Morecambe Bay shrimps, cheese and bacon croissants and venison casserole. They also have four beautifully appointed letting bedrooms available and welcome guests and diners with children.

Penrith lies some five miles from the Eden Valley on the River Eamont. Where the old road from Penrith to Alston crosses the Eden is **Langwathby** - its name meaning 'the settlement by the long ford'. Two prehistoric pathways cross here but the actual name of the village and of its neighbouring settlements suggest a Viking past.

Langwathby has a huge village green which still hosts Maypole dancing on the third Saturday in May. THe green is medieval in origin and would once have been surrounded by wood and mud houses, perhaps to protect cattle but also for defence against border raids. After the Civil War and the growth in prosperity in the late 17th century, these were replaced by stone buildings. The drovers from Scotland passed through here to the market towns of England.

On the opposite side of the river is **Edenhall** and the Church of St Cuthbert. It is said that the Jarrow monks, fleeing from the Viking raids on the east coast, briefly stopped here with St Cuthbert's body before continuing their seven year wanderings. He was finally brought to rest in Durham Cathedral in AD882. Part of the church appears to be pre-Norman though most of it dates from the 12th century.

Nearby is the Plague Cross which stands where there was once a basin filled with vinegar. This acted as a disinfectant into which plague victims put their moey to pay for food from the people of Penrith. The 16th century plague killed a quarter of the village's inhabitants.

Edenhall is particularly famous for the story of the Luck of Eden Hall, once the home of the Musgrave family, now demolished. It refers to a 13th century chalice of enamelled and gilded glass. The chalice is thought to have come from Syria and may well have been brought back by a Crusader. It was a treasured heirloom of the Musgraves for many centuries and is now in the Victoria and Albert Museum in London. According to legend, during a party the family butler went to draw water from nearby St Cuthbert's Well where he found a group of fairies dancing and holding court. When disturbed, they fled, leaving behind the chalice which the butler refused to return to them. As the fairies departed they cursed: *"If ever this cup shall break or fall, Farewell the luck of Eden Hall"*.

The Firs   Penrith   0768 881590

GRIZEDALE FOREST SCULPTURE

Crossing the A686 Penrith to Alston road, and following the course of the River Eden, on the north side is a pretty village called **Winskill**, on the road to Little Salkeld and here you cross the path of the Settle-Carlisle railway once again. In Winskill **The Firs** is a lovely 18th century former farmhouse where Peter and June Toms provide first class bed and breakfast accommodation. A non-smoking establishment, the Toms are happy to cater for children over the age of twelve and offer a warm welcome to all their guests. The four guest rooms are spacious and beautifully decorated, with that extra little touch such as freshly cut flowers in a vase and a welcome tray of tea and biscuits. On fine days you can enjoy a coffee in the garden or sun house, or on cooler days, in the conservatory or cosy guests' lounge. Whatever your needs, The Firs is definitely a home from home treat.

Nearby, in **Little Salkeld** is a fully operational mill powered by a water-wheel. The mill specialises in producing organic, stone-ground flour which is sold locally.It is a short walk by lane from the village to *Long Meg and her Daughters*, a most impressive pre-historic site and one of the largest neolithic stone-circles in the country.

Local legend claims that Long Meg was a witch who, with her daughters, was turned to stone for profaning the Sabbath, as they danced wildly on the moor. The circle is supposedly endowed with magic so that it is impossible to count the same number of stones twice. Another superstition is that Long Meg will bleed if the stone is chipped or broken. The actual name, Long Meg, has been the subject of debate. It has been suggested that 'meg' may simply be a corruption of the word 'magus', meaning a magician.

There are about sixty stones (we dare not attempt to be more accurate than that!) in the oval which is approximately 300ft across. The tallest, Long Meg, is a 15ft column of Penrith sandstone, the corners of which face the four points of the compass. Cup-and-ring symbols and spirals are carved on this stone which is over 3500 years old. The circle is now known to belong to the Bronze Age, but no-one is certain of its purpose. It may have been used for rituals connected with the changing seasons since the midwinter sun sets in alignment with the centre of the circle and Long Meg herself.

In 1725 an attempt was made by Colonel Lacy of Salkeld Hall to use the stones for mile-posts. However, as work began, a great storm blew up and the workmen fled in terror believing that the Druids were angry at the desecration of their temple.

Next to Little Salkeld is **Great Salkeld**, a picturesque collection of 18th century cottages and farmhouses built in the red sandstone that is such a characteristic of this area.Great Salkeld is said to be the birthplace of Dick Whittington. The village church is well known for its massive, battlemented pele tower built in the 14th century. The Norman doorway in the porch is less than a yard wide and its arch has three rows of deeply-cut zig-zags with five heads, one with a crown. The days of the drovers are recalled in the village by the name of its inn, The Highland Drove.

Lieutenant Colonel Samuel Lacy gave his name to the Lacy Caves further along the River Eden from Long Meg. It was he who had the five chambers carved out of the soft red sandstone, possibly as a copy of St. Constantine's Caves downstream at Wetheral. At that time it was fashionable to have romantic ruins and grottos on large estates and Colonel Lacy is said to have employed a man to live in his caves acting the part of a hermit. Alternatively, the caves may have been intended to provide a wine store; Colonel Lacy used to entertain his guests here and there were probably gardens around the caves. You can still see rhododendrons and laburnums which flower every Spring.

On the opposite bank of the river is St Michael's Well, near the supposed site of a village called Addingham which was drowned when the river changed its course in the 12th century. The village church appears to have been an early Christian centre although Viking carvings were amongst some of the stones that were recovered from the river-bed during a drought in 1913. They are now on display at Glassonby. In the 'new' Addingham church the wooden pitch pipe and large stone cross, incised with lines for the ancient game of Nine Men's Morris, are of particular interest. Look out also for the village smithy under an oak tree on the village green and still in use.

The Village Bakery   Melmerby   0768 881515

Midway between Alston and Penrith on the main A686 road is the village of **Melmerby**, home of the famous **Village Bakery**. This award-winning bakery, restaurant and craft gallery was founded by former BBC radio producer Andrew Whitley and his psychotherapist wife Lis who left London in search of the good life in the mid-1970s. Today, they produce a wonderful range of bread, cakes and savouries from certified organic ingredients using a unique wood-fired oven. A greenhouse surrounding the oven is used to propagate plants for the organic smallholding which supplies fresh fruit and vegetables to the restaurant. This is housed in a converted 18th-century stone barn which overlooks Melmerby's extensive village green.

Built around this 13 acre green, Melmerby Hall was a defensive tower, added to in the 17th and 18th centuries. The church, with its tower, was a Victorian building, but the first known rector of the church was in 1332. Melmerby nestles at the foot of Hartside Pass, and the green is dissected by three becks, along which run s a wonderful variety of woodland and wildflowers. Even today, every householder in Melmerby has grazing rights on the green. Horses are grazed more commonly now, but in the past it would have been more usual to see flocks of geese - indeed, there was once a cottage industry here making pillows and mattresses from goose feathers.

The Shepherd's Inn   Melmerby   0768 881217

Between them, the Village Bakery and the village pub seem to have established Melmerby as a small 'foodie's' paradise. **The Shepherds Inn**, run by Christine and Martin Baucutt, is a welcoming establishment full of character and charm. The stone flagged floor, exposed beams, and feature fireplace with a roaring fire in winter all add to the tremendous atmosphere here. The Inn is renowned for its excellent food, winning The Cheese Establishment of the Year award, and recommended by Les Routiers and Egon Ronay. Christine and Martin are also well known for the selection of Cumbrian-made pickles served with the Ploughman's lunches and other dishes. As well as first class food, the Baucutts can provide you with equally high standard accommodation in one of their self catering holiday cottages which are situated in or close to Melmerby.

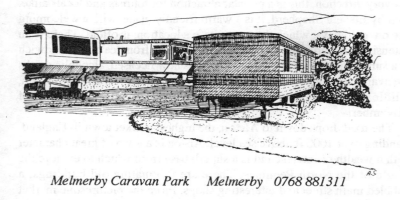

Melmerby Caravan Park   Melmerby   0768 881311

In the heart of the village is **Melmerby Caravan Park**, an ideal touring base. The site is mainly occupied by privately owned static caravans, but there are five pitches for touring vans, with electric hook up points. The toilet block provides full amenities including hot showers, whilst the laundry room has a washing machine, tumble dryer and large sink. With attractively landscaped grounds and excellent facilities, Melmerby Caravan Park is a lovely place to stay while exploring the beautiful surrounding countryside.

Melmerby lies at the foot of the Pennines, and from here, the A686 climbs out of the Eden Valley to the east and the landscape changes suddenly. The road passes Fiend's Fell, close to the highest point in the Pennine Chain which is the summit of Cross Fell, and as you climb, look behind you at superb views of the Eden Valley.

Hartside Café   Alston   0434 381036

At **Hartside Top**, 1904 feet above sea level midway between Melmerby and Alston, you will find **Hartside Cafe**. With spectacular views in every direction, this is a popular attraction for tourists and locals alike. Run by Elsbeth Shepherd, it is a warm friendly place, with a welcoming fire on cold days, which due to the cafe's location, is often! There is an extensive and varied menu providing everything from tea and a sandwich to a substantial hot meal, and as the cafe is now licensed, alcoholic drinks are available. This first class cafe is open daily from 9.30am to 6.30pm, a little later in high season, but closes for the winter at the end of November.

The road drops down to **Alston**, the highest market town in England, standing over 1000 ft above sea level. Alston is a town of great character with a wealth of interest and is a superb base from which to explore the whole of the North Pennines. There are fascinating old buildings, a cobbled main street and interesting shops. From the picturesque market cross narrow lanes radiate out and there are courtyards enclosed by old houses, many having outside staircases. When the houses were first built the living accommodation was upstairs and the animals were kept below. This part of Alston is known as The Butts, a title acquired by the need of the townspeople to be proficient in archery during the times of the border raids.

Gossipgate Gallery   Alston   0434 381806

Here you will discover a beautiful collection of art and crafts at **Gossipgate Gallery**. All the crafts and paintings have been created by artists from Northern England and parts of Scotland and as well as a permanent display, there are regular exhibitions throughout the year on different themes. You are welcome to browse at your leisure and you can sample some of the home-made cakes and biscuits in the gallery Coffee Shop. Should you find the perfect painting for your home, you can purchase it through the Art Purchase Plan, which offers interest free credit for up to 12 months on items up to £1000.

An unusual feature of Alston is the number of watermills in and around the town and the mill-race was once the central artery of the old town. At the newly opened High Mill visitors can see the enormous Smeaton water wheel. The tall spire of St. Augustine's Church is a local landmark, and its churchyard contains a number of interesting epitaphs, as well as affording wonderful views of the South Tyne Valley. Nent Force, a waterfall, is where John Smeaton, builder of the Eddystone Lighthouse, built a five-mile underground canal tunnel - the Nent Force Level.

Alston Moor was once the centre of an extremely important lead-mining region, one of the richest mining areas in Britain. Lead and silver were probably mined on the moor by the Romans, but it reached its peak in the early part of the 19th century when vast quantities of iron, silver, copper, zinc and other materials were mined by the London Lead Company, which employed thousands of workers at Nenthead. The quaker company was a pioneer of industrial welfare and built the model village of Nenthead to house the miners, introducing compulsory education, public baths and other benefits to its community.

Nent Hall   Alston   0434 381584

Close by, on the edge of Alston, on the A689 towards Stanhope, you will find a first class hotel, **Nent Hall**. Situated in this remote and unspoilt area of beautiful countryside, here you will discover a taste of luxury and comfort. Proprietors Eric and Dorothy Peacock bought Nent Hall in 1989, but it was only in mid-1991 that they felt satisfied with the extensive refurbishments and added extensions that the hotel had undergone. It is immediately apparent that their efforts have been successful and Nent Hall is now a first class hotel which has earned a two star RAC and AA rating, plus the English Tourist Board's four crown commended award. The bar area is cosy and full of character with flagstoned floors, a feature stone fireplace and a granite bar surface. Known as the Coach House Bar, the room was built using mainly materials from a local derelict barn. The lounge and dining area are relaxing and comfortable, showing the class and style that the Peacocks have brought to the place. The food is first class and ranges from tasty bar snacks to a full dinner menu. The guest rooms are all magnificently decorated and with their own individual character, whilst providing all the modern amenities you would expect. One room has been specially adapted for the disabled, and two others boast four poster beds, one with a sunken bath, making it ideal for honeymooners or that special romantic occasion.

Lowbyer Manor   Alston   0434 381230

Approximately five minutes away from the centre of Alston, on Hexham Road, you will find **Lowbyer Manor**, a delightful 17th century former manor house which is now a first class country house hotel. The original layout of the building has been retained and the exposed beams and inglenook fireplace in the cosy guests' bar add to the hotel's historic character. Proprietors Peter and Margaret Hughes provide accommodation in twelve attractively furnished en-suite bedrooms, offering every modern comfort, and in the lovely Derwent Restaurant you can sample a mouthwatering a la carte menu. With the Pennine Way close by, Lowbyer Manor makes an ideal touring and walking base for this lovely area of the High Pennines.

Alston's Information Centre is in the waiting room of the town's station, now served by the South Tynedale Railway. Visitors can take a scenic ride along the narrow-gauge steam railway hauled by little vintage engines, to Gilsland Halt on the Northumberland borders.

The remote, grey stone hamlet of **Garrigill** lies in a deep ravine three miles from the source of the River Tyne at the foot of Cross Fell. It can be reached from the B6277 Barnard Castle road or by foot along the Pennine Way, four miles south of Alston. The church was refurbished in the 18th century but parts of it are over 700 years old. The bell is said to have been the dinner bell at Dilston Hall in Northumberland, in the days of the Jacobite Earls of Derwentwater.

George and Dragon   Garrigill   0434 381293

In the heart of the village is the **George and Dragon Inn**, a 17th-century former coaching inn with stone flagged floors, open log fires and a wonderful atmosphere. The establishment is owned by Brian and Jean Holmes who serve a fine selection of hand-pulled ales and a range of excellent value bar meals. They also have a number of comfortably appointed letting rooms available and a small bunkhouse for walkers, but it is unsuitable for young children.

Shield Hill House   Garrigill   0434 381238

Shield Hill House is a delightful country guesthouse near Garrigill (For accurate directions, telephone the owners Phil and Catherine   Bradley on 0434 381238). This charming family-run establishment takes its name from the old Scottish word *shieling* meaning a summer grazing ground. It stands on the side of the South Tyne Valley with spectacular views southwards towards Cross Fell. Each bedroom has a private bathroom, and there is a comfortable lounge stocked with toys, games and books. Delicious English breakfasts and four-course dinners are served each morning and evening, and the guesthouse is open all year round except at Christmas.

Coming back down into the Eden Valley again, to the right of the A686 is the attractive and unspoilt fellside village of **Gamblesby**, dominated by a large village green which protected the cattle during the winter months. You can still see the village stocks, with iron shackles instead of traditional wooden ones.

The road continues along the valley, past **Lazonby** and on to picturesque **Kirkoswald**, once a thriving market town where you can still see a small cobbled market place and some very fine Georgian buildings. The village derives its name from the church of St. Oswald. Oswald was the King of Northumbria who, according to legend, toured the pagan North with St. Aidan in the 7th century.

Kirkoswald also has a ruined 12th century castle, formerly the home of the Featherstonehaugh family and, although not open to the public, it can be seen from the road and footpath. In 1210 a licence was received from King John to fortify the original structure and enclose the extensive park. The castle was later destroyed by Robert the Bruce in 1314 but was rebuilt and extended in the late 15th century. THe whole site covered three acres with the courtyard surrounded by a massive wall and a main gate with a drawbridge over the moat. The castle's splendour is due to the efforts of Thomas, Lord Dacre but after his death in 1525 the panelling, stained glass and beamed ceilings were transferred to Naworth and the castle became a quarry. Today it is still protected by a wide moat and the great turreted tower rises above the remains of the vaulted dungeons.

One of Kirkoswald's most splendid buildings is the College, its name recalling the days when St. Oswald's was a collegiate church. The two-storied house with its sloping-ended roof was originally built in 1540 as a pele tower and converted into the college for priests in the 1520's. The manor house opposite has a particularly attractive entrance front in sandstone, which was added in 1696.

If you are looking for first class self catering accommodation in beautiful surroundings then **Howscales**, just outside Kirkoswald, is the ideal place. Owned and run by Colin and Elaine Eade, Howscales is a retired farmstead providing five luxurious cottages, tastefully converted from the old barns and byres. Ideally situated as a touring base, the cottages are set amongst some of the finest scenery and countryside you will find. The cottages are for non-smokers only and provide excellently equipped and beautifully furnished accommodation. All are centrally heated and carpeted throughout, but maintain their charm and character with the honey pine furniture complementing the original beamed ceilings and wood panelling. Three of the cottages, The Granary, Geltsdale and Ravendale have their bathroom and bedrooms on the ground floor and the lounge and kitchen/dining area on the first floor, whilst the other two, Hazelrigg and Inglewood have all the rooms on the ground floor. All five have a superbly equipped kitchen with every modern convenience and there are laundry facilities available, with washing machine, tumble dryer and drying racks. An added touch on your arrival is the provision of dish-cloths, toilet rolls, bin-liners, washing-up liquid, rubber gloves and an apron, all useful essentials to get you started. Kirkoswald is less than two miles away, with a post office, general store, first class butchers, two churches, a garage and three pubs which all serve food, ensuring you have everything you need for a perfect holiday.

Howscales   Kirkoswald   0768 898666

Between the villages of Kirkoswald and **Armathwaite** are the Nunnery Walks which start at a Georgian house built in 1715, on the site of a Benedictine Nunnery founded during the reign of William Rufus. Narrow footpaths cut into sandstone cliffs along the deep gorge of Croglin Beck and pass through beautiful woodland to reveal exciting waterfalls. The walks are open to the public during the summer months.

Croglin, an unspoilt village nestling below the fells of North Cumbria, is famous for the legendary vampire that appeared here in 1895. The legend claimed that it only laid to rest after it had attacked a sleeping girl. It is here that you will find **The Robin Hood Inn**, a deceptive building whose rather plain external appearance belies its true character.

97

This is apparent as soon as you walk through the door, with welcoming open log fires, extraordinary beams and bygone memorabilia all creating a very special atmosphere. As well as serving fine ales and an excellent range of bar meals, your friendly hosts the Hunters, also provide three spacious tastefully decorated guest rooms. The inn is open all day and there is always a plentiful supply of tea and coffee for the thirsty tourist.

The Robin Hood Inn   Croglin   0768 86227

In the quiet village of Ainstable, heading towards the A6, you will find **Heather Glen Country Hotel**, an elegant late Victorian mansion standing in over two acres of beautiful grounds with its own small beck running through. Inside the hotel, the cosy bar area gives you the opportunity to chat with the locals and sample the excellent value bar meals, and the magnificent dining room/restaurant with its oak panelled walls provides the perfect setting in which to enjoy the extensive a la carte menu. An impressive staircase with feature window leads to the five beautifully furnished en-suite guest rooms where you are sure to waken refreshed, relaxed and ready to explore.

Heather Glen Hotel   Ainstable   0768 86219

While you are in Ainstable, visit the Eden Valley Woollen Mill, where you can watch cloth being made.

The Fox and Pheasant Inn   Armathwaite   06992 400

It is a delightful walk from here along the eastern bank of the River Eden to Armathwaite. A particularly fine sandstone bridge crosses the river in the village and from it there is a lovely view of Armathwaite Castle.In this picturesque, unspoilt village stands the impressive **Fox and Pheasant Inn**. This former 18th century coaching inn run by Mo Starkie and her son Ian, is full of character with exposed beams, original flagstone floors and roaring log fires for those chillier days. There is a Victorian addition of a separate guests' lounge and restaurant where Ian provides an excellent, varied menu as well as daily blackboard specials to choose from. The eight letting bedrooms are cosy and individual, with one reputedly haunted by a highwayman. With ample off-road parking, The Fox and Pheasant is ideally situated for fishing enthusiasts and for touring the beautiful Eden Valley, the Lakes and the Yorkshire Dales.

Nearby, the main A6 Penrith to Carlisle road passes through the attractive village of **High Hesket**, about eight miles outside Carlisle, where there is a first-rate roadside inn, the **Cross Keys Tavern**, which is owned and personally run by Alan and Helen Hutchison. Many of the original features of this 200 year-old Georgian pub have been retained (including its splendid inglenook fireplace), helping to create an atmosphere which is truly relaxed and welcoming. As well as a first-class pint of beer, Alan and Helen serve a varied selection of excellent value bar meals including steaks, fish, salads, jacket potatoes and special children's meals. The tavern also has also a well-equipped games room and an attractive children's play area to the rear.

South of High Hesket on the west side of the River Petteril, the village of Calthwaite is also well worth a visit. Renowned locally for the dairy which was a major source of employment for many years, this delightful village was the Royal Forest of Inglewood, a fact substantiated by the many local names such as High Oaks and Low Wool Oaks and Roe deer can still be seen here today. The appropriately named Thiefside, just east of Calthwaite, was the site of the gallows where poachers and sheep stealers were hanged.

Cross Keys Tavern   High Heskett   06974 73238

CHAPTER FOUR

Carlisle to the Borders

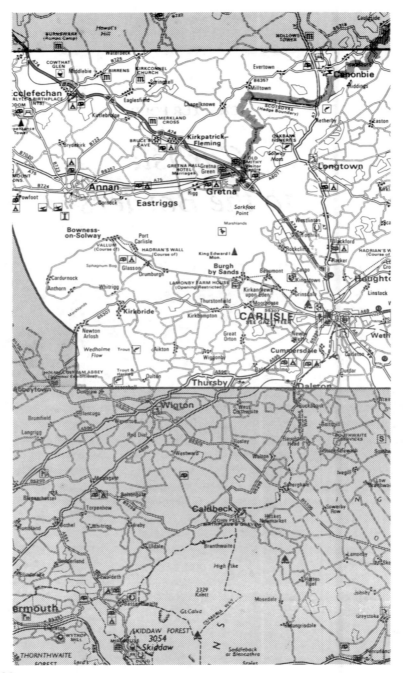

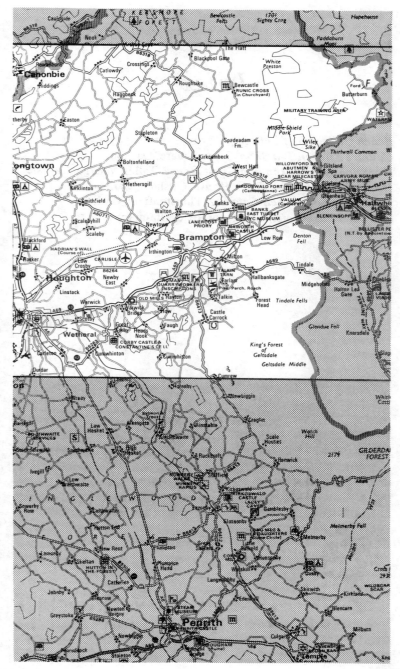

CHAPTER FOUR

Index

Carlisle Cross

Carlisle to the Borders

Bewcastle

CHAPTER FOUR

Carlisle to the Borders

The area around Carlisle has changed its allegiance to Scotland and England so often in the last 800 years that many of the inhabitants could be forgiven for not knowing whether to wear the thistle or the rose. This is Border Country, a wild and lonely, evocative landscape that sets the scene for so many of Sir Walter Scott's historical novels.

But Carlisle's history is more than mere romance. This was a major strategic city on the Border, whose military past still seems to haunt it - from the Roman and Pictish battles to the skirmishes with the Scots and Jacobite rebels. There has been a castle at Carlisle at least since 1092 when William Rufus first built a palisaded fort. Almost certainly there was a fortress, probably on the present site, before roman times, for the name 'Carlisle' comes from the celtic 'Caer Lue', meaning 'hill fort'.

Carlisle Castle

The Norman castle was originally built of wood but, during the Scottish occupation in the 12th century, King David laid out a new castle with stone taken from Hadrian's Wall. You can still see the 12th century keep enclosed by masive inner and outer walls although they have been much altered over the years.

107

The present castle dominates the skyline of this fascinating city. Entered through a great 14th century gatehouse, complete with portcullis, and with a maze of vaulted passages, chambers, staircases, towers and dungeons, it is everything a real castle should be. Look out for the 'licking stone' and the fascinating carvings in one of the prisoners' cells showing pictures of mermaids, knights, boars and crucifixes.

Carlisle Castle was besieged for eight months during the Civil War by the Parliamentarians under General Leslie. When the Royalists finally capitulated, Leslie began repairing the castle and the walls. The Puritans were no respecters of Britain's ecclesiastical heritage; stone from six of the eight bays of the Cathedral was used for the repairs and the building of block-houses for the Puritan troops.

Partially for this reason, Carlisle Cathedral is now one of the smallest cathedrals in England but it has many interesting features, including an exquisite East Window, considered to be one of the finest in Europe. Below the beautifully painted wooden ceiling of the choir, with its gold star shimmering against deep blue, are the carved, canopied choir-stalls with their medieval misericords. These wonderful carved beasts and birds include two dragons joined by the ears, a fox killing a goose, pelicans feeding their young and a mermaid with a looking glass.

In the north transept is the superb 16th century Flemish 'Brougham Triptych' which was originally in Cologne Cathedral. In the 19th century it was brought to Brougham Chapel near Penrith. The altar piece was later restored by the Victoria and Albert Museum in London and is now on permanent loan to Carlisle. It is a beautiful, intricate piece with delicately carved figures depicting scenes from the life of Christ.

It is hard to believe that this is where Edward I solemnly used bell, book and candle to excommunicate Robert the Bruce. It was here also that the church bells were rung to welcome Bonnie Prince Charlie in 1745. It is claimed that after the suppression of the Jacobite rebellion the bells were removed for their treason and only replaced in the 19th century!

Visit the Prior Tower if you can, although an appointment is usually necessary. On the first floor of this 15th century pele tower is a wonderful forty-five panel ceiling incorporating the popinjay crest and arms of the Prior Senhouse. The 16th century Prior's gatehouse leads to a narrow lane called Paternoster which is named after the monks reciting their offices.

To understand fully the story of Carlisle, you have to go to **Tullie House**, the city's outstanding museum; indeed, if you do nothing else in Carlisle, don't miss this place. Skilful displays and interpretive techniques make the city's history into an exciting adventure, and paint a vivid and dark picture of the Debatable Lands, as this border region was called.

Carlisle Cathedral

The museum's centrepiece is its story of the Border Reivers who occupied the lands from the 14th to the 17th century, with a law - or rather, a lack of it - unto themselves, being neither English or Scottish, unless it suited them to pledge, unscrupulously, allegiance to one or the other. These lawless, unruly people raged inter-family warfare with each other, decimating the lives of the local people, carrying out bloodthirsty raids in which victims lost their homes, their cattle, their possessions and often their lives, too.

The horrific stories of the Reivers have been passed down through the generations in the Border Ballads, and many of the Reivers family names are still known - the museum even offers a genealogy service, so that you can trace your ancestry back to these people. The definitive Reiving story has been told in The Steel Bonnets by George MacDonald Fraser, author of the Flashman books.

Tullie House also has an extensive collection of Roman remains from both the city and the Cumbrian section of Hadrian's Wall. Carlisle is a great centre for Roman history. What is now the city centre was initially a military base for the Petriana regiment. 'Luguvalium', as it was called, became a major Roman civilian settlement with fountains, mosaics, statues and centrally-heated homes.

Like many great medieval cities, Carlisle was surrounded by walls. The best view of these is in a little street called West Walls at the bottom of Sally Port steps, near the Tithe Barn. The walls date from around the 11th century and remained virtually intact until the 19th century. When the castle was under siege, the Sally Port allowed an individual to 'sally forth'. It was later used for access to the Tithe Barn to avoid paying city tolls. It is unusual to find a tithe barn within a city wall but this exception was probably made because of the Border raids. The barn dates from the 15th century and was used to collect and store taxes, or tithes, destined for the priory. Close by is St Cuthbert's Church, the official city church of Carlisle, housing the Lord Mayor's pew. Although the present building dates from 1778, there has been a church of St Cuthbert on this site since the 7th century. St Cuthbert was Bishop of Carlisle in AD680. It is a charming Georgian building with several interesting features including a moveable pulpit on rails.

The old Town Hall, now an excellent Tourist Information Centre, dates from the 17th century and once housed the 'Muckle Bell', an alarm bell which, it was claimed, could be heard eleven miles away. The bell is now housed in the **Guild Hall Museum**. The museum was originally built by Richard of Redeness in 1407 and is a prime example of an unspoiled medieval building. It provides an ideal setting for illustrating the history of both the Guilds and the City. Several rooms are devoted to

110

Guild Hall Museum

creating the atmosphere of trade Guilds such as the shoe-maker, the butcher and the glover. Particularly impressive is the collection of 18th-century Guild silver-ware. Displays also feature other items relating to the history of Carlisle and include a magnificent iron-bound Muniment Chest dating from the 14th century. Conducted tours of this remarkable Guildhall are available using a "Time Machine" audio guide.

Not far from the museum is the **Citadel Railway Station**. The first railway to Carlisle opened in July 1836 and Citadel Station, which opened in 1850, was to house seven different railway companies whose coats of arms are still displayed on the facade. So elegant was its interior - and much of it remains - that Carlisle was known as the 'top hat' station. Today it is still an important station; Intercity trains from Glasgow and London now link with lines to Dumfries, Tyneside, West Cumbria and Yorkshire, and it is, of course, the northern end of the famous Settle-Carlisle Railway line.

The line of Hadrian's Wall runs through Carlisle following the northern rim of the River Eden. The Wall was built as a great military barrier across the narrowest part of Britain, from the mouth of the Tyne in the east to Bowness-on-Solway in the west. Guarded by forts at regular intervals, it was built between AD122-128 following a visit by the

111

Emperor Hadrian who saw the military infra-structureas insufficient to withstand the combined attacks of northern barbarians. Originally much of the western side was built from turf, but by AD163 this had been replaced by stone. The wall was finally abandoned in the late 4th century.

Eagle Crag

Some of the best remains are to be seen at **Birdoswald**, a Roman fort that guarded the bridge carrying the Wall over the River Irthing at Willowford. Birdoswald is set high on a plateau with magnificent views over the surrounding landscape. The fort has a particularly well preserved eastern gate. It would originally have covered five acres and may have been the base for 500 cavalry or 1000 foot soldiers. The site at Birdoswald is now open to the public. It belongs to English Heritage, who have carried out much excavation work and opened a Visitor Centre which brings the history of this site to life, from the early Roman days, through the middle ages and the border raids, to the romanticism of the Victorians. In 1850 Henry Norman, an enthusiastic archaeologist, extened the farmhouse, built the tower and began the excavation works to the fort walls and gates. Recent excavations have uncovered the fort's granaries and west gate with evidence of early post Roman occupation. Birdoswald is unique; at no other point along Hadrian's Wall can all the components of the Roman Frontier system be seen in such a small area. A fine stretch of the Wall runs from Birdoswald to Harrow's Scar Milecastle which stands at the top of a steeply-wooded slope overlooking the river.

East of Birdoswald is **Gilsland**, where there is one of the best preserved milecastles on the Wall. Standing on a grassy slope above Poltross Burn, it is 10ft high in places. Gilsland is also known for its sulphur spring and there was once a convalescent home for miners and shipyard workers here. It is now owned by the Co-operative Society and people still drink the waters as a cure for arthritis and rheumatism. Near the spring is the Popping Stone, traditionally where a man popped the question to his lover. It was here that Sir Walter Scott successfully proposed to Charlotte Carpenter.

About 1/2 a mile out of Gilsland, standing on a hilltop, is **Howard House Farm**, a charming period farmhouse over 130 years old. Situated amidst some of the most spectacular stretches of Hadrian's Wall, it commands a marvellous view of the Irthing Valley and makes an ideal touring base for this beautiful area so rich in history. This is a friendly working farm with a small flock of the rare breed Jacob sheep, and cattle. The farmhouse has been lovingly restored to retain its charm and character, and oozes warmth and comfort with open log fires in period fireplaces. This E.T.B. 2 crown commended establishment provides a full breakfast and wholesome farmhouse dinner, with vegetarian dishes available if required.

Howard House Farm   Gilsland   06977 47285

Following the course of the River Irthing back towards Carlisle, two miles north east of **Brampton** is Lanercost Priory, an impressive red sandstone ruin set in secluded woodland. The Priory was founded in 1166 by Robert de Vaux and built largely of stone from the Roman Wall. During 1306, Edward I spent six months at the Priory recuperating after his skirmishes with the Scots. Lanercost is well preserved and its scale is a reminder that it was a grand complex in its heyday. However, the Priory suffered greatly in the Border raids of the 13th and 14th centuries. It was finally disbanded at the Dissoltuion of the Monasteries but in 1740 the ruined nave was restored to form what is now one of the most splendid parish churches in the country. It is worth going inside to admire the William Morris glass.

Across the River Irthing from Lanercost stands **Naworth Castle**, situated on a rocky cliff above a deep, wooded ravine. It formed the setting of Walter Scott's 'Lay ofthe Last Minstrel'. The castle was built in 1335 in its present form by Lord Dacre as an important border stronghold. The castle passed through the female line to the Howard family after the last Lord Dacre was killed as a child, improbable as it might seem, falling off his rocking horse!

Naworth is now owned by the 12th Earl of Carlisle, and has recently begun to open to the public. Its supreme glory is the Great Hall hung with french tapestries and guarded by four unique heraldic beasts holding aloft their family pennants. The Long Gallery extends for 116ft and was used as a guardroom. It now houses an interesting collection of paintings, many brought together by the 9th Earl, George Howard. He entertained many pre-Raphaelite painters here but the only existing example is Burne-Jones' 'Battle of Flodden' - the rest were destroyed by a fire in 1844. In the courtyard there are some intriguing medieval latrines!

The ancient market town of Brampton was the headquarters of Bonnie Prince Charlie in his seige of Carlisle in 1745. When the city surrendered to the Scots the mayor and aldermen came to Brampton to present him with the keys to the city of Carlisle. A few months later, on his defeat, six of his supporters were hanged on a tree on the south side of the town. The tree survived until the last century and in its place there now stands a monument commemorating this event.

Brampton actually dates back as far as the 7th century, and was originally sited a mile northwest of its present position. On the departure of the Romans from the area, the settlement grew. The present town was created by Thomas de Multon, Lord of Gilsland, in the early 13th century. The octagonal **Moot Hall** in the market place, with its handsome clock tower, is Brampton's most striking building. It is also where you will find the Tourist Information Centre, on the upper floor. The present hall was built in 1817 by Lord Carlisle but there has been a Moot Hall here since 1648. The iron stocks at the foot of a double flight of external stairs were last used in 1836.

Just off the market square is St Martin's Church which was rebuilt in 1878. It was designed by Philip Webb, a member of the pre-Raphaelite brotherhood, who requested that stained glass should be installed. Climb

114

up to the wooded mound for a magnificent view of the Solway Plain and the distinctive Scottish mountains on the Galloway coast.

Oakwood Park Hotel, on Longtown Road, just outside Brampton, makes an excellent base for touring the Borders, and the Lake District and is situated within a mile of Hadrian's Wall. Standing in secluded grounds, with its own tennis court, this impressive Victorian residence provides comfortable accommodation in five en-suite guest rooms all with TV and hot drinks facilities. The atmosphere is warm and welcoming with open log fires in the dining room and drawing room. There is a cosy lounge bar where guests can relax with a drink before sampling the excellent traditional dinner menu. There are also two self-catering cottages available close to the hotel, both of which sleep up to four and provide first class facilities.

Oakwood Park Hotel   Brampton   06977 2436

To the north of Brampton is **Walton**, a small, pretty village with lime trees around its green. Nearby, in the beautiful Irthing Valley, is **Castlesteads**, where a garden has been created among trees and flowers on the site of a Roman camp.

South of Brampton are Gelt Woods, lying in a deep, sandstone ravine carved by the fast-flowing River Gelt. By the river is an inscribed rock called Written Rock which is thought to have been carved by a Roman Standard Bearer in AD207. From Gelt Wood it is a delightful walk to Talkin Tarn, where the lake in the Country Park has been popular for water-sports for over 100 years. Legend has it that beneath the surface of the lake there is a submerged village destroyed by a wrathful god and that in certain light you can still see the ruins below.

Enjoying a charming location in the lovely Cumbrian village of **Talkin**, you will find the **Hare and Hounds Inn**. This historic 18th century coaching house was once used as a stop-over by monks on their

115

way from Armathwaite to Lanercost Priory. This is a welcoming establishment where you can sample fine cask-conditioned ales and tasty home-cooked meals. The Tarn Lounge provides a cosy relaxing atmosphere with exposed beams, open fires and soft lighting. The Coats of Arms Bar is a special feature with stained glass windows around the bar. At the end of the day, you can retire to one of the comfortable guest rooms, one of which has a four-poster bed.

Hare and Hounds Inn   Talkin Village   06977 3456

A little further south is the village of **Castle Carrock** lying among beech trees below the fells with an old pub and stone cottages. An ancient settlement, archaeologists have found several pit-dwellings in the hills above the village and and a skeleton of a man with a drinking cup in a cairn at Greenwell.

Between Castle Carrock and Carlisle is **Wetheral**, above the River Eden, over which runs an impressive railway viaduct carrying the Tyne Valley Line. Wetheral Parish Church lies below the village beside the river and contains a sculpture by Joseph Nollekens, of the dying Lady Mary Howard clasping her dead baby. St Constantine was the local patron and the church is dedicated to the Holy Trinity, St Constantine and St Mary. Constantine died as a martyr in AD657 and a life-sized statue of him can be seen in the grounds of Corby Castle.

During the reign of William Rufus one of his barons, Ranulph Meschin, founded a priory for Benedictine monks at Wetheral above the red-rock gorge of the River Eden. It was a dependency of the Abbey of St Mary at York and the Prior and the monastery served the church and domestic chapel of Corby Castle. All that remains now is the gatehouse, but the grounds of Corby Castle are open to the public and provide some very pleasant woodland walks.

It is well worth visiting the remarkable Norman church of St Leonard at nearby **Warwick**, which consists of a restored nave and chancel with a curiously buttressed apse and a splendid arch leading into a modern vestibule. Warwick's other church, St Paul's, is reputed to have been commissioned by a wealthy Carlisle man who took umbrage at a sermon preached at St Leonard's.

On the north side of Hadrian's Wall, towards the Scottish border, is Longtown, the last town in England. Its position, on the River Esk and so close to the border, has influenced its history from earliest times. The Romans occuoed this land, and they were followed by other conquerors. The legendary King Arthur attempted to organise the Northern Britons against the pagan hordes who tried to settle and control this territory. In the 6th century the mighty battle of Ardderyd was fought here, and acoording to legend, 80,000 men were slain.

Until 1750 Longtown was a small hamlet of mud-dwellings. Dr. Robert Graham, an 18th century clergyman, proposed the building of the Esk bridge, which was completed in 1756 and it was this venture that led to Longtown's establishment as a bustling border town. These days it has some fine individual buildings and broad, tree-lined terraces of colour-washed houses.

Riverside at Wetheral

On the outskirts of Longtown, just off the A6071, is **Arthuret Church**. The earliest records of the church date from 1150 and it was originally served by the monks of Jedburgh. But it is thought that the earliest church here may hvae been founded by St Kentigern in the sixth

117

century, and most recently, research has led people to believe that King Arthur was actually interred here, after his last battle, Camboglanna, was fought a few miles east of Longtown at Gilsland.

The present church, dedicated to St Michael and All Angels, was built in 1609, financed by a general collection throughout the realm, which James I ordered after a report that the people of Arthuret Church were without faith or religion. The people that he referred to, of course, were the infamous Reivers, ungoverned by either English or Scottish laws

Arthuret Church

Archie Armstrong, favourite Court Jester to James I and later Charles I, is buried in the churchyard which also contains an unusual stone cross. It consists of two parts of an early medieval wheel-head cross clamped together onto a tapering shaft with 19th century decorations.

In 1745 another army marched through Longtown; this time it was Bonnie Prince Charlie and his men, making a bid for the English crown.They crossed the River Esk at Riddings and stayed at Riddings Hall.

To the north of Longtown is the parish of **Kirkandrews**, long associated with the Grahams of Netherby Hall, where Sir Walter Scott wrote 'Young Lochinvar'. The grounds of the hall are sometimes opened to the public in Spring, when the daffodils are in bloom. The beautiful church at Kirkandrews was connected to Netherby Hall by a suspension bridge, which is now privately owned. Built in 1637, it contrasts strongly with the 15th century pele tower nearby, the tower having been built for safety during the attack, whereas the church was built after peace came to the area.

From Kirkandrews, Hadrian's Wall continues along the Solway coast to **Bowness**. Many of the sandstone cottages around here contain stones from the Wall. Some of these stones can easily be identified, such as the one let into a barn near the King's Arms. In the porch are two old bells, dating from 1611 and 1616. It is alleged that in 1626 some Scotsmen crossed the Solway and stole the Bowness church bells. They were spotted, chased and forced to lighten their boats by throwing the bells overboard.

At one time sailing boats made their way by a canal from **Port Carlisle** to the heart of the city of Carlisle. Boats were towed to the city (taking 1 hour 40 minutes), enabling Carlisle to be reached within a day by sea from Liverpool. The canal was later replaced by a railway which brought many Scandinavian emigrants through Carlisle on their way to the USA. The building of the Bowness railway viaduct altered the deepwater channels, causing Port Carlisle to silt up and the railway was abandoned but its old course can still be traced.

For real home from home self-catering accommodation you need look no further than **Beach Cottage** at Bowness-on-Solway. Owner Jane Simmons has made this lovely 18th century stone built cottage into a delightful holiday retreat. There are two bedrooms, one double and one twin, plus a sofa bed in the lounge which can sleep two. The living room is cosy and welcoming with a range with open fire and children are well catered for in the small "den" where they will find books and games to keep them amused. Situated right on the shore, the cottage enjoys lovely views across the Solway Firth and in summer you can watch the fishermen going out with their traditional Ha'af nets.

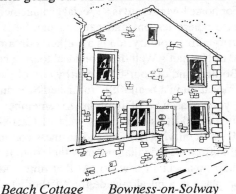

Beach Cottage   Bowness-on-Solway   06973 51745

The Solway Firth coast is an area of tiny villages with fortified towers standing as mute evidence to the Border struggles of long ago. These villages were the haunts of smugglers, wildfowlers and half-net fishermen. What is particularly special about this coastline is its rich birdlife. At the isolated village of **Rockcliffe**, on the north bank of the Eden, the marshes are famous for migratory birds. If you are there at the right time of year, the long skeins of migrant geese, passing overhead on their way to the Arctic, are a never-to-be-forgotten sight.

On 7th July 1307, the body of King Edward I was laid out in the church at **Burgh-by-Sands**. He was already a dying man when he left Carlisle to march against his old enemy, Robert the Bruce. A monument to Edward was erected on the marshes and a later monument still marks the spot. The Church of St Michael dates from 1181 and was constructed entirely of stones from a fort on the Roman wall. Of particular interest is the fortified tower built for defence against the Border raids, which has 7ft thick walls. The tower can only be entered through a strong iron grill; this is possibly the earliest surviving example of a fortified church.

The church in the village of **Kirkbampton**, though restored in 1882, was originally Norman and let into the chancel-wall are even older stones taken from the Roman wall.

This coastline is the setting for Walter Scott's novel, 'Red Gauntlet', and the fortified farmhouse by the roadside at Drumburgh is said to be the 'White Ladies' of the novel. Further along the coast is **Glasson**, an important Nature Reserve and the centre of the half-net fishing industry.

Lovers of true country holidays will find the perfect self catering accommodation at **Lakeshore Lodges** in nearby Thurstonfield. Situated on the banks of a 25 acre natural lake, this is a fisherman's paradise, with a plentiful supply of rainbow and brown trout to be hooked and free use of a boat if required. For horse lovers there is a special arrangement with Stonerigg Riding Centre where lessons and hacking can be booked, whilst the beautiful surrounding countryside is a walker's dream. Located at the western end of Hadrian's Wall this is an ideal touring base for the North Lakes, the Borders and of course the nearby city of Carlisle. With first class accommodation in a beautifully furnished Scandinavian bungalow to return to, you are assured of a holiday to remember.

The village of Thurstonfield lies five miles west of Carlisle and between 1870 and 1930 was a thriving farming and business community. Almost completely self-sufficient, the villagers grew their own fruit and vegetables and used their own wells for water. At that time, although illegal, cockfights took place in a pit alongside the Methodist chapel, originally built in 1861, which still serves a congregation today.

South of Thurstonfield at the junction of the A595/596 is the village of Thursby which takes its name from Thor, the Saxon god of Thunder whose temple was said to have been nearby at Kirksteads. A focal point of the village is St. Andrew's church which dominates the skyline and it is here in the graveyard that the body of Rev. Mason lies, a former curate of Thursby whose granddaughter was the famous Mrs. Beeton, writer of the classic book on 'Household Management'.

Lakeshore Lodges   Thurstonfield   0228 576552

Just east of Thursby lies Dalston, a delightful and unspoilt country village close to Carlisle. Here in the main square you will find **Country Kitchen**, a traditional tea shop run by Julie Dixon where you can enjoy home cooking at its best. Country Kitchen is a cosy, friendly establishment with a roaring fire on cold winter days tempting locals and tourists alike to pop in and sample the freshly baked gingerbread or Cumberland currant cake with a warming drink. There is always a soup of the day, a roast of the day, a vegetarian dish, as well as two other daily specials on the blackboard, all made using local produce. You can even take some homemade bread away with you as a tasty memento.

Country Kitchen   Dalston   0228 711431

Lying on the banks of the river Caldew, Dalston became a thriving cotton industry in the late 18th century, thanks to George Hodgson of Manchester, who used the river as the source of power for the flax mill and four cotton mills that were established here. The local economy was sustained still further by the emergence of a forge and two corn mills.

At the eastern end of the village square, stands St. Michael's church, believed to date back to Norman times, which can be approached via a memorial lychgate. One of the few red brick buildings to be found in the village is the Victorian chapel which stands somewhat hidden between several Georgian houses along the village green.

CHAPTER FIVE

North Lakeland

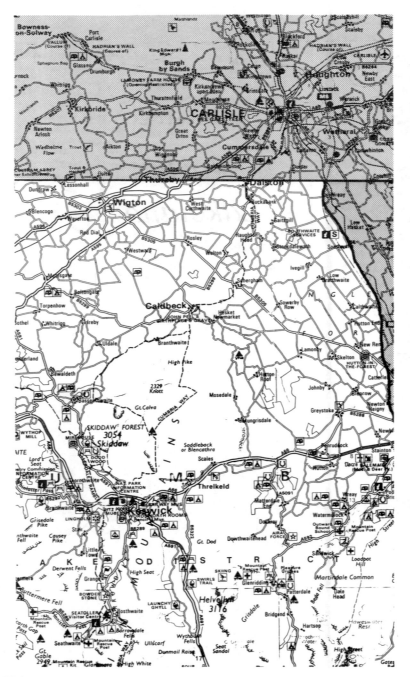

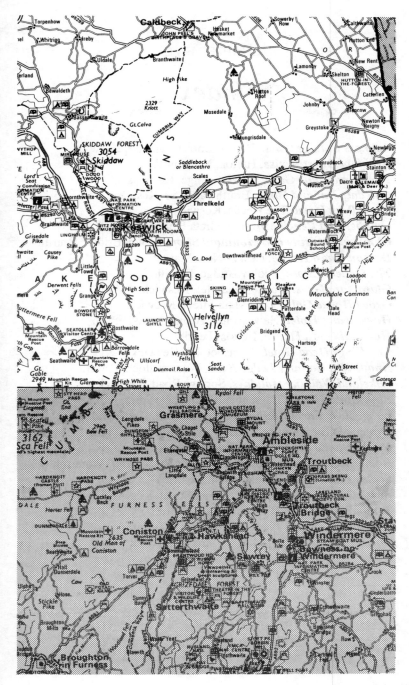

CHAPTER FIVE

Index

Moot Hall, Keswick

North Lakeland

Stonethwaite in Borrowdale

CHAPTER FIVE

North Lakeland

The northern Lake District, to the north, east and west of Keswick, is for many enthusiasts, classic Lakeland, the scenery dominated by the rounded, heather-clad slopes of the Skiddaw range to the north of Keswick, and the wild, craggy mountains of Borrowdale and the Central Fells to the south. But despite this area's popularity, there are many hidden places to discover which are off the beaten track.

North of Skiddaw, towards Carlisle, lies an area of countryside formerly covered by the ancient Forest of Inglewood. Now it is farmland with isolated hamlets across which a dense network of quiet lanes and trackways are spread, dotted with attractive villages such as **Westward**, **Rosley** and **Ivegill**.

Sedbergham is the largest village, a scattered settlement containing several 18th century farmhouses. Legend says that it was founded in medieval times by a hermit - one William Wastell - who made a clearing in the forest with his four supporters and established the village.

The most famous village in this area is **Caldbeck**, because of its associations with John Peel, the famous huntsman who lies buried in the churchyard. Peel was Master of Hounds for over fifty years and was immortalised by his friend John Graves, who worked in a local mill making the grey woollen cloth mentioned in the song, *"D'ye ken John Peel with his coat so grey?"*

With its picturesque church, village green, cricket field, pond and blacksmith's forge, Caldbeck has all the ingredients of a picture postcard village. There has been a church here since the twelfth century, one of only eight in England to be dedicated to St. Kentigern. The other seven are also to be found in the north of Cumbria, where Kentigern, a bishop in the Strathclyde area of Scotland, spent his time in exile.

Until two hundred years ago Caldbeck was an industrial village, with corn mills, woollen mills and a paper mill all powered by the river. Priest's Mill, built in 1702 by the Rector of Caldbeck, next to the church, was a stone grinding corn mill, powered by a waterwheel which has now been restored to working order. It is open to the public, and has an accompanying mining museum and a collection of old rural implements. The mill buildings are home to a gift shop, craft workshops, and a tea-room - one of Cumbria's best - on the top floor.

Denton House   Hesket-New-Market   06998 415

Just one mile from Caldbeck is the peaceful and attractive village of **Hesket-New-Market**. The village is surrounded by beautiful country-side and is within easy reach of the Caldbeck Fells, Carrock Fell and The Swineside Valley. On the edge of Hesket-New-Market you will find

130

Denton House, a charming guest house run by Margaret Monkhouse. Set in its own lovely gardens, Denton provides six comfortable letting rooms and a guest lounge with TV and video. Pets and children are made welcome, with cots and highchairs available if required. As well as a full breakfast, Margaret is happy to provide packed lunches and evening meals by prior arrangement.

Between Caldbeck and Penrith, north of the A66 and Ullswater is another quiet part of Cumbria. **Greystoke**, on the B6288, is notable for its magnificent collegiate church dating from the 13th century, once the home of a college of canons, and as big as a small cathedral. There is a wonderful East Window with much 13th century glass and, in the Lady Chapel, a figure of Madonna and Child carved by a German prisoner-of-war.

Tymparon Hall   Newbiggin   07684 83236

About a hundred yards from the church stands the Plague Stone where, during medieval times, coins were left in vinegar in exchange for food for the plague victims. An ancient Sanctuary Stone, now concealed behind a grille, marks the point beyond which fugitives could claim sanctuary.

The village has a fine green, some attractive houses and Greystoke Castle, now an imposing private house. There are several race-horse stables in the area.

Nearby, and worth visiting, is **Hutton-in-the-Forest**, the beautiful historic home of Lord and Lady Inglewood, featuring fine collections of furniture, paintings and tapestries, with a walled garden, topiary terraces and a lovely woodland walk. Hutton-in-the-Forest is about 6 miles to the north west of Penrith, on the B5305 Wigton Road.

A few miles south is **Newton Reigny** on the River Petteril, north west of Penrith. It takes its name from the de Reigny family who had possessions in this part of Cumbria in the 12th century. The church of St John, though restored, dates from the 14th century, and two names carved on a beam near the chancel are reputed to be those of two local carpenters,

John Atkenson and Henere Bymert, who constructed a new roof in 1585.

A couple of miles off Junction 40 of the M6 through the village of Newbiggin, you will find **Tymparon Hall**. This 150 acre working sheep farm is run by Margaret and Jim Taylor who have been providing bed and breakfast for the past fifteen years. A sweeping driveway leads to this 18th century manor house, where the beautifully stocked garden is a sight to behold and the warm friendly welcome will have you relaxing the minute you arrive. The attractively decorated guest rooms are spacious and offer excellent facilities, whilst downstairs there is a cosy guest lounge with an open fire. Margaret serves hearty farmhouse breakfasts as well as splendid three course evening meals, and can even provide packed lunches for those wishing to explore the surrounding country side.

Just south of the A66, heading towards Pooley Bridge and the north east end of Ullswater, is an area of gently undulating countryside where the Lakeland mountains ease into the Eden Valley. Here you will find such charming villages as **Yanwath** and **Tirril**, both of which have Quaker connections. Yanwath Hall, reputed to be the finest manorial hall in England, was the birthplace of the Quaker Thomas Wilkinson, and in Tirril is an old Quaker Meeting House (now a private house).

Cumbrian Marine and Mountain   Pooley Bridge   07684 86401

Nearby is **Dalemain Historic House and Gardens**. Its impressive Georgian facade is just that - it was added on to the Elizabethan house in the eighteenth century. The house itself cannot be said to belong completely to any one era, as it has evolved through a variety of architectural fashions over the centuries. This makes it all the more fascinating to explore; some parts are a confusion of winding stairs and passages, others a series of grand public rooms, housing a rich collection of portraits and fine furniture. Dalemain is surrounded by spectacular gardens with many rare plant species on display.

Pooley Bridge is a charming Lakeland village within the National Park boundary, at the tip of Ullswater, which many say is the Lake District's most beautiful lake. Its oldest building is part of Holly House which dates back to 1691 whilst the 'bridge' of the village's name was begun in 1763. Before Bridge was added, the name Pooley meant 'pool by the hill' and was derived from the pond which existed behind the Sun, and Dunmallard, the cone-shaped hill on the other side of the river. In the centre of Pooley Bridge today, you will find **Cumbria Marine and Mountain,** a friendly store run by Adrian North and Ian Proud. Here they retail and mail order outdoor clothing, handle boat repairs and winter storage, run a chandler's and boat yard, as well as actually selling boats. The building they occupy is appropriately enough, a former boat building site in Pooley Bridge.

The General Store   Pooley Bridge   07684 86266

The General Store in Pooley Bridge is run by a lovely couple, John and Anne Goth. The store has been serving the needs of locals and tourists for the past 30 years and has a reputation for friendly service and value for money. Here you will find everything you need, ranging from a full Post Office facility and newsagents', to everyday groceries and confectionary. Holiday-makers are well served with a comprehensive range of camping supplies and outdoor clothing including Lakeland Weatherwear, plus the additional bonus of a bicycle hire and repair service. Whatever your needs, it is immediately apparent that customer satisfaction is the main priority at Pooley Bridge General Store.

Along the southern edge of Ullswater is one of the Lake District's most famous hotels, **Sharrow Bay**, with the most breathtaking views onto Ullswater. For most, this is a place for a once-in-a-lifetime treat, and the hotel is more suited to a romantic weekend way than a family holiday - something that is definitely worth saving for! For details, telephone 07684 86301.

On the opposite edge of the lake the views are beautiful too, and it was on the northern shores of Ullswater, at Glencoyne Wood, that William Wordsworth, on a bleak and breezy April day, noticed the brilliance of the wild daffodils, an experience that he shared with the world in one of the most quoted poems in the English language; "*I wondered lonely as a cloud....*"

Close to Glencoyne at Watermillock is another beautifully situated hotel, **Rampsbeck**, a country house hotel standing in 18 acres of parkland and gardens on the shore of Lake Ullswater. This delightful 18th century hotel offers first class accommodation in an idyllic and tranquil setting. The bedrooms are spacious and attractively furnished and most have views of the Lake or hotel gardens. The candlelit dining room is the beautiful setting for a cosy intimate dinner, where the mouthwatering menu is imaginative and varied and has been awarded two AA restaurant rosettes. Afterwards you can relax in front of an open log fire in the elegant drawing room which overlooks the Lake, or on fine evenings take a stroll around the beautiful gardens.

Rampsbeck Country House Hotel   Watermillock   07684 86442

Also in Watermillock, between Pooley Bridge and Glenridding on the A592, is **Ullswater Caravan, Camping and Marine Park**. Run by the Dobinson family, it is an ideal base for a camping or self-catering holiday. The tastefully converted farmhouse and farm buildings provide nicely furnished, well equipped holiday homes, each sleeping up to six people, whilst the spacious caravan site has several luxury six berth static caravans to let. There is plenty of space for visitors, tourers or tents and the first class site facilities include shower and toilet block, licensed bar, a children's playground, general store, public telephone, and a snack bar. Visitors can also make use of the Dobinson's extensive Boat Park and Marina which is a mile from the campsite.

Ullswater Caravan Park   Watermillock   07684 86666

Staying in Watermillock, which is only about ten minutes away from Penrith, is **Knotts Mill Country Lodge**, a charming, bed and breakfast establishment run by Jane Jones. This former sawmill was rebuilt as a guest house in the 1960's and has since been refurbished to provide first class accommodation. Standing in its own grounds set back from the road, Knotts Mill enjoys a peaceful location, with lovely views of the fells. There are nine en-suite bedrooms, four of which are ground floor units and one has been adapted for wheelchair users. The dining room is licensed and Jane provides dinner as well as free morning coffee and afternoon tea for her guests.

Knotts Mill Country Lodge   Watermillock   07684 86472

About a mile to the north of Watermillock is the village of **Dacre**. The village church in Dacre occupies a site of a former monastery which was mentioned by the Venerable Bede in his accounts of Cumberland in the

135

8th century. Fragments of masonry are reputed to have come from the monastery and four carvings of bears in the churchyard are probably of Anglo-Viking origin.

Dacre Castle is a 14th century pele tower, a type of fortified house or small castle common in Northern England. This was the seat of the Dacre family, Catholic Earls of Cumberland and its turrets and battlements have walls which are eight feet thick. Leonard Dacre took part in the ill-fated 'Rising of the North' in 1589. The estate passed to the Earls of Sussex who restored the castle in 1675 and whose Coat of Arms can still be seen.

Going south from Dacre, between Ullswater and Haweswater, is the Lowther Estate. On its edge is the delightful village of **Askham**. Its name means 'the place of the ash trees' and it has a large green surrounded by old houses and cottages. From Askham you can look across the River Lowther to the facade of Lowther Castle; the building is now only a shell, most of it having been demolished in 1957, but it was clearly once a grand place; after one visit Queen Victoria is reputed to have said that she would not return to Lowther Castle as it was too grand for her.

The ancestral owners of the castle were the illustrious Earls of Lonsdale, statesmen and sportsmen. The most famous is perhaps the Fifth Earl (1857-1944), known as the Yellow Earl because of the colour of the livery used on his private carriage. He was the first President of the Automobile Association and permitted his family colours to be used by the Association. The Earl was also a patron of amateur boxing and the Lonsdale Belt emerged from his interest. One of the earlier Lords, better known as Wicked Jimmy, was a famous ghost at the castle. The yellow flag of the Lonsdales can be seen in Lowther Church.

There are two Lowther villages, **Lowther Newton**, close to the centre of the estate, which was built in the late 17th century to replace an existing village, and **Lowther**, to the east , a remarkable model village designed by the 18th century architect, Robert Adam.

Holywell Country Guest House   Helton   0931 712231

South of Askham is **Helton**, another attractive and secluded village with several 17th and 18th century houses. Anne and Rob Hunt are a friendly, enthusiastic couple who enjoy welcoming guests into their home at **Holywell Country Guest House** in Helton. Having undergone extensive refurbishment, this part 17th and part 19th century house offers first class accommodation comprising three bedrooms, one of which is en-suite, and a private guest bathroom. Downstairs you can relax in comfort in your own private sitting room and enjoy the superb views across the Lowther Valley, and outside you can admire the mature garden and magnificent fells around Haweswater. Anne and Rob welcome children over the age of ten, but out of consideration to other guests, please no pets and no smoking.

Beckfoot House　　*Helton*　　*0931 713241*

Helton, 'town on the side of a hill', is midway between the northern tips of Ullswater and Haweswater, and close by is Moor Divock, an archaeological site of stone circles and cairns. Close to the village is the delightful country guesthouse, **Beckfoot House**. This large and elegant residence was originally constructed in 1773 with later additions in the early-1800s and in 1892. (To mark the centenary of the later extension, one of the rooms has been made into a Victorian museum containing interesting prints, clothes and memorabilia.) On entering, visitors are welcomed into a half-panelled hall with an open fire and a magnificent stately staircase. The dining room is panelled in English oak and has a superb French oak fire surround and a unique collection of ceramic tiles depicting scenes from Shakespearian plays. The sitting room also features a delicate cornice constructed by craftsmen brought specially from Italy. Beckfoot House is owned and personally-run by Lesley and David White who provide a friendly family atmosphere in this charming unspoilt corner of the Lake District. Its location is ideal for walks over the fells to Ullswater

137

and Haweswater, the home of a pair of golden eagles. The guest bedrooms all have private shower/bathrooms, colour televisions and fine views over the three-acre garden which contains a sundial with the unusual inscription: '*At Beckfoot here amid the flowers, Reckon none but happy hours*'.

The road southwards continues via **Bampton-by-Penrith**, close to an ancient settlement, to Haweswater.

Haweswater Hotel   Haweswater   0931 713235

The **Haweswater Hotel** near Bampton stands in a magnificent position alongside beautiful and secluded Haweswater. Situated midway along its eastern bank, this fine country hotel looks out across the lake towards the breathtaking landscape of Laythwaite Crags. The building was originally constructed in 1937 and has been owned and personally run by Mr and Mrs Rockell since 1989. Recently refurbished, the public rooms have a charming homely atmosphere and tremendous views over the surrounding Lakeland countryside. The sixteen comfortable guest bedrooms all have hot and cold washbasins and good modern facilities. Three also have balconies overlooking the lake. First-class cuisine is served in the hotel's elegant dining room and there is also a pleasant bar, lounge and terrace.

In Bampton Church you can see a painting of Mardale Church, which was in the village of Mardale, drowned when Haweswater, an artificial lake, was contructed and filled as a reservoir to serve the needs of the City of Manchester.

Above Haweswater runs The High Street, a Roman road and now one of the most popular fell-walks in the Lake District. It overlooks the remote and lovely **Blea Tarn** and the lonely valley of **Martindale**, a cul-de-sac valley south of Ullswater, where England's last remaining herd of wild red deer is often visible from the surrounding fells.

One of the nicest ways to cross from one side of Ullswater to the other is by lake-steamer, which links Pooley Bridge with the little village of Glenridding at the opposite end, and at the foot of the Kirkstone Pass. Regular sailings through the summer months allow a boat trip to be combined with a particularly beautiful walk along the eastern shores of Ullswater from Howtown to Sandwick and Patterdale.

Close to the junction of the A592 Glenridding to Penrith road which hugs the shores of Ullswater and the A5091 is the spectacular waterfall, Aira Force, now in the ownership of the National Trust. This famous waterfall was the setting for the romantic and tragic story of Emma, who fell in love with a renowned knight called Sir Eglamore. He had to leave her to follow the Crusades. As the months lengthened into years and he had not returned, Emma became so distraught that she started to sleep-walk to Aira Force where she eventually met her tragic death. On his return, the grief-stricken Sir Eglamore became a hermit and lived by the waterfall for the rest of his days.

Scales Farm   Threkeld   07687 79660

Leaving Ullswater behind you, continue along the A5091, through **Matterdale** with its little old church dating from 1573, to the junction with the A66, where a right turn would take you to Penrith and a left turn heads for Keswick, passing through the lovely Lakeland hamlet of **Scales**, on the slopes of Blencathra, one of the highest mountains in England. Here you will find **Scales Farm**, a rather special bed and breakfast establishment. The proprietors Alan and Sheila Appleton are a very friendly, professional couple who take pride in the service and amenities they offer their guests. There are five exquisitely furnished double and twin rooms situated in a tastefully converted barn area with skylight windows. All are self-contained with en-suite bath/shower and have colour TV, hot drinks facilities, and a bar fridge, ensuring complete comfort for all who stay here.

A little further along the same road is **Threlkeld**, a village of great charm, famous for its annual sheep-dog trials. It is the ideal starting point for a number of mountain walks, including an ascent of Blencathra, one of the most exciting of all the Lake District mountains.

Between Threlkeld and Keswick lies St John's Vale, where you will find Castlerigg, a remarkable Neolithic circle of 38 stones which commands a superb view of the surrounding fells. Whatever the purpose of the monument, it was a strategic view-point where priests or princes could survey the fell-country. Not far away on High-Rigg, overlooking the Vale, is the little chapel of St John, built close to the site of a 13th century hermitage.

Cumberland Pencil Museum   Keswick   07687 72116

Keswick is the largest town within the Lake District Park and its stunning position, surrounded by the mountains of Skiddaw and Borrowdale, and on the shores of Derwent Water, makes it one of Britain's most poular inland holiday resorts.

The volcanic rocks of Borrowdale, newer than the Skiddaw slate group, are rich in minerals, and the discovery of one of the strangest, graphite, led to the development of the pencil industry in Keswick. In the fascinating **Cumberland Pencil Museum** you can discover the history behind this everyday object, the pencil, through machinery displays and video shows. Children will like the drawing corner with a free drawing competition to enter, as well as the brass rubbing which always proves popular. This unique museum, which follows the story of Cumberland Graphite and the development of the pencil manufacturing industry in Keswick, is of interest to all of us since we have all used these pencils at some time or other. You can pick up a memento of your visit in the Museum Gift Shop which of course sells pencils, in addition to numerous other items.

In the centre of Keswick the busy little main street is full of shops and cafes, filled with traditional Lakeland fare, the best of which is to be found at **Bryson's Bakery**, whose Lakeland Plum Loaf is famous all over the world, and is still made to a secret recipe. The old Moot Hall is now the Tourist Information Centre, and packed with useful maps and guides for walkers as well as plenty of information about the local attractions and accommodation. All the T.I.C.s in the area are listed at the back of the book.

Art lovers and visitors looking for that special gift should call in to **Grove House Gallery** on Keswick's Main Street. Run by Sarah Holmes, the gallery specialises in original Lakeland landscapes in oils and watercolours by top artists such as Arthur Blamires and Jack Beddows. There are various limited edition prints by the likes of Judy Boyes and John Carver as well as some locally handcrafted items and hand thrown pottery. The listed building features two original wells, one where you can pause to throw a coin and make a wish, the money then going to help local charities. Afterwards take time to browse around the array of crafts, jewellery and vast selection of mineral specimens, many of which are collectors pieces.

Grove House Gallery   Keswick   07687 73942

Next to the Town Hall stands **The Wild Strawberry**, a delightful tea room and gallery run by Michael Stimson and Brian Twigge. A non-smoking environment, the tea room is charming and traditional, with local green slate floors, beamed ceilings and boasts the best view of the Moot Hall Clock Tower. Here the emphasis is on tasty home-cooked snacks and cakes, accompanied by a choice of quality teas and coffees to a backdrop of soothing classical music. After sampling the lovely home-made scones, or the naughty but nice Sticky Toffee Pudding, you can browse around the gallery which is full of unusual cards, gifts and crafts, specialising in fine art posters and limited edition etchings.

The Wild Strawberry   Keswick   07687 74399

Mid-way between the shores of Derwentwater and the old Market Square, stands the impressive **Crow Park Hotel**. Owned and personally run by a welcoming couple, Ian and Margaret March, the hotel offers first class accommodation at very reasonable prices. The attractively furnished guest rooms are all en-suite and provide excellent facilities, whilst downstairs you can relax in the cosy bar with a drink and admire the many attractive prints which adorn the walls. In the comfortable dining room the extensive table d'hote menu offers excellent, freshly prepared, home-cooked food, accompanied by a carefully selected wine list.

The Crow Park Hotel   Keswick   07687 72208

A short walk out of the town centre, along the Lake Road and past the bustling lakeside promenade, will take you to the popular Century Theatre and Friar's Crag. This famous view of the Derwent Water and its islands, now National Trust property, formed one of John Ruskin's early childhood memories.

Although the centre of Keswick is busy, it has quieter places. Just behind the central shopping area is a little park alongside the River Greta. Not far away the fascinating Fitz Park Museum and Art Gallery has an unusual stone xylophone and an important collection of manuscripts by Wordsworth and Southey.

Lynwood House   Keswick   07687 72398

Enjoying a quiet location just a few minutes walk from the centre of Keswick is **Lynwood House**, on Helvellyn Street, a charming non-smoking guest house run by Basil and Joyce Clement Evans. Nothing is too much trouble for this friendly couple who go out of their way to make thir guests feel welcome. There are five well equipped bedrooms all with colour TV and beverage making facilities, whilst downstairs the pretty dining room provides a comfortable setting for the hearty breakfast provided each morning. Home-cooked evening meals are available at a very reasonable price, with large portions being the order of the day.

Swiss Court Guest House   Keswick   07687 72637

As you come along the main road into Keswick, not far from the town

143

centre, on Bank Street you will find **Swiss Court Guest House**, a friendly and welcoming establishment run by Teresa Salingre. Although within easy reach of the main shopping area, Swiss Court enjoys a peaceful location in a quiet part of the town. The very reasonably priced accommodation comprises seven guest rooms, all en-suite, with TV and hot drinks facilities. The beautifully decorated dining room is light and airy, with a large bay window and numerous pot and hanging plants providing a lovely setting for you to enjoy the full English breakfast Teresa prepares each morning.

Brockhole

Walking enthusiasts will find **Lakeland Walking Holidays** the perfect way to enjoy their favourite leisure pursuit while absorbing the outstanding beauty of the Lake District. The holidays are run by Ian McQueen, a highly experienced local guide who organises high and low level walks to suit both the novice and the more experienced walker. For your week's holiday you can choose to stay in either a country house hotel or a town guest house and the overall tariff will include dinner bed and breakfast, six packed lunches and transport to and from walks where applicable. With everything organised for you, all that remains is to pack the essential clothing and equipment, before setting off to enjoy the wonders of the Lake District. Ian can be contacted on 07687 73628.

Keswick also has a close association with the National Trust. Canon Rawnsley, the local vicar, was one of the founder members of the Trust, which he helped to set up in 1895. Rawnsley fought for years to get Brandelhow Woods and Fell for the Trust, raising £7000 in five months. This was the first National Trust property in the Lake District, and it has grown since then to include most of the Central Fell area. However, despite the help of Rawnsley's contemporaries such as William Morris, John Ruskin and Thomas Carlyle, he couldn't prevent Manchester

Corporation from flooding the two natural lakes of Thirlmere, which submerged the old road and hamlets of Armboth and Wythburn, and the bridge which had joined the two lakes where Wordsworth and Coleridge used to meet each other. Wythburn Church survives, a favourite spot from which to start the climb up Helvellyn.

The Kings Head Hotel   Thirlspot   07687 72393

Nearby, at the foot of Helvellyn on the A591 Grasmere to Keswick road at **Thirlspot**, stands **The Kings Head Hotel**, an impressive 17th century coaching inn.   Careful refurbishment has provided modern refinements whilst retaining the hotel's original charm and character. Here you can enjoy a good selection of well-kept, traditional ales and the excellent menu offers a wide range of tasty dishes to appeal to every palate.   Accommodation is provided in nineteen well-equipped, en-suite bedrooms, all furnished in keeping with the hotel's character. Your welcoming hosts are the Sweeney family who own another popular inn, The Traveller's Rest in Grasmere and their experience in the hotel business is self-evident here, in the friendly atmosphere, the tastefully furnished rooms and the excellent service.

Three miles north of Keswick on the A591 (the old Carlisle road), you will come to **Long Close Farm**, Underskiddaw; a mid-18th century farmhouse sheltering below Dodd Wood, set in five acres and enjoying spectacular views south west across the Derwent River - towards Newlands Valley, Grisedale Pike and Bassenthwaite Lake. Long Close Farmhouse provides first class bed and breakfast accommodation in three attractive double bedrooms with friendly and courteous service, and is open all year for holidays. Travellers to and from Scotland find it a convenient and delightful resting place within the Lake District National Park. Completely separate whilst adjoining the farmhouse and sharing its outlook is self-catering cottage accommodation that houses 4-6 persons comfortably, and is fully equipped for long or short stays, where children and pets are welcome.

Long Close Farm   Underskiddaw   07687 72851

If you leave Keswick heading west on the A66, towards Cockermouth, you will come to the village of Braithwaite. On the way, visit Lingholm, home of Lord and Lady Rochdale. It has very impressive gardens and woodland, open to the public through the summer, and great views. Beatrix Potter's family used Lingholm for many years as a holiday home and it crops up in many of the writer's tales. The woods here were Squirrel Nutkin's home. Just north, at Fawe Park, is Benjamin Bunny country, and to the south, at Newlands Valley, Mrs Tiggy Winkle lived up the side of Cat Bells.

Coledale Inn   Braithwaite   07687 78272

When you reach **Braithwaite**, through the village and over a stone bridge is the **Coledale Inn**, a 'hidden place' well worth seeking out. Set high above and overlooking Braithwaite, this is still the locals' pub and the busy Georgian and Victorian bars reflect its popularity. The Coledale is run by Peter and Susan Mawdsley and their two sons, Geoffrey and Michael who like to remember their guests by sending them Christmas cards. An idea of the esteem in which they are held is shown by the fact that previous landlords return here to spend their own leisure time. The Inn was built originally in 1824 as a woollen mill, changed identity to a pencil mill and eventually became licensed premises during the mid 1900's. Set well away from passing traffic and with Grisedale Pike on the doorstep, it is situated on the Coledale Round and there are many other walks in the area. The garden in front of the house can be used for eating and drinking and is where Mr. Mawdsley sometimes holds barbecues. The house has been sensitively adapted for modern-day use yet is full of Victorian prints, furnishings and antiques; open fires bring extra cheer during the winter months. The twelve-bedroom accommodation is all en-suite and the rooms have colour TV and coffee making facilities. The basic tariff is for bed and breakfast only, but lunches and evening meals are served daily and packed lunches are available on request. Residents have their own dining room and reading lounge, but meals are served in either of the two bars. This is a free house serving 'Real Ales', (including a good local one), and an inexpensive range of wines is available by the carafe or bottle. Well known for the high standard of its food, the Coledale serves starters, light meals, main courses, salads, desserts, farmhouse cheeses and a childrens' menu as well as having a daily 'Chef's Special'. Hot chocolate, tea and coffee (plain or liqueur) are also on the menu.

Lingholm Gardens

Maple Bank   Braithwaite   07687 78229

Also just past Braithwaite on the A66 you will find **Maple Bank**, a charming country guest house run by a friendly and helpful couple, Beryl and Russell Birkett. Standing at the foot of Whinlatter Forest, Maple Bank boasts magnificent views across to Skiddaw and is very close to Whinlatter Visitor Centre. The first class accommodation comprises seven en-suite guest rooms, all with colour TV, electric blanket and beverage making facilities. The spacious dining room is tastefully furnished and provides a comfortable setting in which to enjoy the substantial English breakfast served each morning. Evening meals are available if required and guests here can also make use of the facilities at Braithwaite Bowling and Tennis Club.

Link House   Bassenthwaite Lake   07687 76291

The lovely hamlet of **Dubwath** nestles in the beautiful, unspoilt area around Bassenthwaite Lake. Here you will find **Link House**, a charming Victorian country house run by friendly hosts, Brian and May Smith. The

148

Friar's Crag

beautifully furnished accommodation with lovely antiques and period pieces, provides eight en-suite bedrooms all with colour TV and hot drinks facilities. The spacious reproduction Victorian conservatory is the perfect place to relax with your morning coffee, whilst the lounge has an air of cosy intimacy with its open log fire. The elegant dining room provides the perfect setting for the fine English breakfast and to complete your stay there is an excellent five course dinner with accompanying wine list, prepared by Mary each evening.

The Borrowdale Gates   Grange in Borrowdale   07687 77204

At the southern end of Derwent Water is Cat Bells, one of the most beautiful ridge-walks in all England. A good way to set off for such an excursion is to take the motor-launch from Keswick to **Hawse End**, where the ascent begins. Following the path along the ridge, you will descend again to the ancient hamlet of **Grange in Borrowdale**. Here stands a luxurious country house hotel, **The Borrowdale Gates**. Newly renovated to a very high standard by proprietors Terry and Christine Parkinson, the hotel boasts outstanding views towards Castle Grag and the Glaramara mountain range. The warm relaxed atmosphere in the lounges and bar are enhanced by open log fires and lovely antique furniture, whilst the elegant dining room provides the perfect setting in which to savour the first class breakfast and dinner menus. Terry prepares an imaginative and varied selection of dishes to appeal to every palate, accompanied by a carefully chosen wine list. To complete your stay there are 23 tastefully furnished en-suite bedrooms all offering picturesque views of this lovely part of the Lake District.

Borrowdale is a brooding, mysterious valley, steep and narrow with towering crags and deep woods. You can wander past the famous Castle Crag, climb the Bowder Stone or, best of all, take a choice of paths through the thickly-wooded hillside over to the hamlet of Watendlath. The view from Ashness towards Keswick, across Derwent Water, with the little hump-backed bridge in the foreground, is one of the most photographed in England.

Ashness Cottage   Borrowdale   07687 77244

A little way up the road from Ashness Bridge you will find the beautifully situated **Ashness Cottage.** Nestling in 3 acres of woodland and paddock high on the hillside, the cottage boasts magnificent views over Derwentwater. Run by a very friendly couple Patsy and David Hamilton-Wright, this charming cottage is a haven for walkers and nature lovers. There are four comfortable and very reasonably priced guest rooms and a small guest lounge, but no TV since reception is so poor. An added attraction is the Hamilton-Wright's two pet donkeys and Henrietta and Harriet, the sheep!

A couple of miles along the valley, at the bottom of Honister Hause, the pass which leads over to Buttermere, is Seatoller. From here begins the famous and well-trodden track, via Seathwaite, over Styhead Pass to Scafell Pike, England's highest mountain.

Glaramara   Seatoller   07687 77222

151

Enjoying an idyllic location at Seatoller, close to the foot of Honister Pass and eight miles from Keswick, **Glaramara** is a purpose-built chalet style house offering first class holiday accommodation. The house is owned by Countrywide Holidays Association, a non-profit making organisation established 100 years ago who pioneered walking and special interest holidays. There are 13 Countrywide properties in the British Isles all offering very reasonably priced accommodation for one or more nights. At Glaramara you are surrounded by spectacular mountain scenery, with the like of Scafell Pike and Hopehill Head beckoning the enthusiastic fell walker, whilst meandering streams and footpaths offer a more leisurely alternative to the less energetic and many local attractions are within easy reach You can call the house direct to book accommodation, or for special interest and walking holidays telephone 061 225 1000.

Watendlath

The regular bus service between Seathwaite and Keswick describes itself, with some justification, as the most beautiful bus ride in Britain. It certainly is lovely and gives access to the whole of Borrowdale.

CHAPTER SIX

South Lakeland

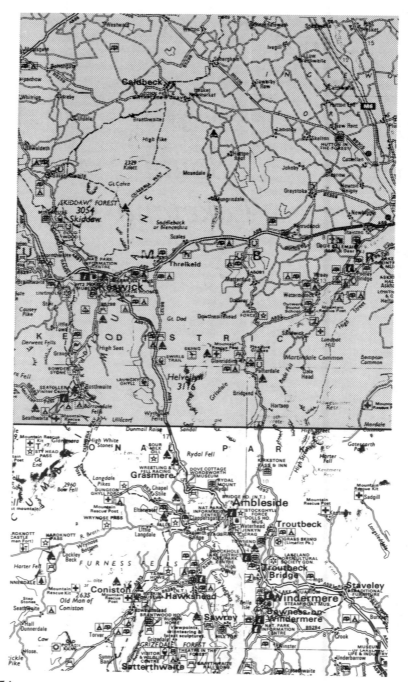

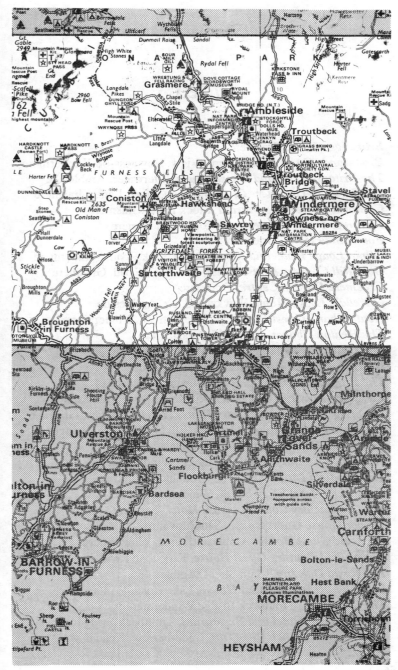

CHAPTER SIX

Index

Dove Cottage

South Lakeland

Kentmere Hall

CHAPTER SIX

South
Lakeland

The southern part of the Lake District is Cumbria's best known and most popular area, with the main resort towns of **Windermere** and **Bowness**, and the picturesque villages with all their literary associations. The great English poet, William Wordsworth, spent all his life in this area and loved to walk for miles through the countryside, with Helvellyn in the background, drawing inspiration for some of his greatest work from his surroundings.

Coleridge, De Quincey, Southey and Ruskin also spent much of their lives around the lakes of Grasmere, Windermere and Coniston. Beatrix Potter, creator of Peter Rabbit, Squirrel Nutkin and other famous characters, lived at Sawrey, and Arthur Ransome based all of his Swallows and Amazons books around Coniston. The list goes on, and it is easy to understand how the landscape has inspired such creativity in these and so many other writers and artists.

Grasmere Gardens   Grasmere   05394 35255

The focal point of Wordsworth Country is the picturesque village of Grasmere, in its particularly lovely mountain setting, close to its very pretty lake of the same name and with craggy hills all around.

159

Grasmere is a small village and gets extremely busy, but it is delightful to walk around and worth braving the crowds before you head for the more hidden places of South Lakeland. One road winds its way through the village, past St Oswald's Church, where William Wordsworth and many members of his family are buried in the churchyard. The aroma of baking gingerbread is quite mounthwatering as you leave the churchyard and pass Sara Nelson's famous gingerbread shop in what was once Grasmere's school house.

A trip to **Grasmere Gardens** is a must. The main studio at the Gardens was beautifully constructed three years ago out of timber and Westmorland Greenslate, although there has actually been a garden centre on this site for more than 100 years. The Centre has been carefully laid out, with wide paths offering easy access to buggies and wheelchairs, and there are also toilet facilities for the disabled. There are four acres in total, with the plants displayed in garden settings to enable the visitor to visualise them at home. The Centre specialises in Ericaceous plants such as azaleas, conifers and heathers, which are particularly suited to the acid soil of the area. Everything is labelled and should you require it, there is plenty of help available from the trained horticultural staff. However, Grasmere Gardens is more than just a centre for plants, it is a veritable garden gift store. Visitors can browse through the main studio at their leisure, admiring the large selection of garden furniture and barbecues for sale. There is also a wide range of Royal Doulton china and fine crystal to choose from, or attractive displays of dried and silk flowers to catch your eye. You will even find country clothing here, not to mention maps and numerous books. Once you have made your purchases, you can relax and unwind in the comfortable coffee shop, where light snacks and refreshments are available all day. Altogether Grasmere Gardens has something for everyone and makes an interesting alternative trip.

Heaton Cooper Studio   Grasmere   05394 35280

Lovers of Lakeland art will find a veritable haven at **The Heaton Cooper Studio**. It houses a permanent exhibition of work by W. Heaton Cooper R.I. and his father, A. Heaton Cooper (1863 - 1929), both of whom are recognised as the foremost artists of the area. It is a real family business, with Julian Cooper, the grandson of Alfred Heaton Cooper, and son of renowned sculptress, Ophelia Gordon Bell, inheriting the artistic talent. The family now offer the largest collection of Lakeland prints and greeting cards in the area which has been built up over the last 50 years. There are various Ophelia Gordon Bell sculptures on show, as well as a supply of signed copies of books by W. Heaton Cooper, containing many illustrations of his work.

Craglands of Grasmere   Grasmere   05394 35283

Craglands of Grasmere is a unique, quality clothing shop, which appeals to locals and tourists alike. Situated only a short distance from Wordsworth's cottage, it is run by Christine Shaw, a textile designer turned retailer, who sells her beautiful designs and colours of tweeds both as metred fabric and ready made skirts. She also has a wide range of top quality lambswool and cashmere knitwear and mohair capes, which co-ordinate perfectly with the subtle shades of the tweed. To complete the outfit, there is an extensive selection of costume jewellery and silk scarves of all colours, and for the men, a range of classic knitwear and fine tweed ties. Christine also runs a huge mail-order business, marketing her quality garments all over the world.

Close to the coach and car park, on Stock Lane, **Cumbria Carvery** is an excellent place to pause for a while and absorb the scenic beauty. Run by two friendly families, this lovely tearoom and restaurant with its stucco walls and charming wooden pews and tables, offers a range of hot meals and light refreshments throughout the day. In the evening the place takes on an elegant informality with white and green table linen and a varied menu of tasty home-cooked food, both English and Continental. The pretty tables and chairs outside give the Cumbria Carvery a European cafe air, and signify it as an excellent meeting place for locals and tourists alike.

Cumbria Carvery   *Grasmere*   *05394 35005*

No trip to Grasmere is complete, of course, without a visit to the **Wordsworth Museum** and **Dove Cottage**, where William and his sister Dorothy lived from 1799 - 1808. In 1802 William married Mary and she came to join the Dove Cottage household. Coleridge and De Quincey often came to stay - in fact, one gets the impression that they came perhaps just a little too often, indulging in quantities of opium and swelling numbers uncomfortably in this rather small house, where newspaper lined the walls for warmth and economy, and for much of their time here, the Wordsworths could afford little more to eat than porridge. This must have been an eccentric household, and the guided tour of Dove Cottage paints a very clear picture of their lifestyle, with a little insight into the unusual relationship between Dorothy, William and Mary Wordsworth. In the museum, the Wordsworth Trust's collection is inspiringly pre-sented, and includes original Wordsworth manuscripts, letters exchanged between Wordsworth and his friends, and extracts from the original of Dorothy's journals. Give yourself half a day to visit this and Dove Cottage.

Grasmere is a good central point to explore both north and south Lakeland, and there are some fine walks from here into Easedale, over to Grizedale and Patterdale, or over Greenup Edge into Borrowdale. Once you have walked out of the village and begin to climb out of the valley, you will be away from the congestion, instead rewarded by the most breathtaking views across the lake of Grasmere and its neighbour, Rydal Water.

Boasting one of the best locations in the Lakes, **Gold Rill Country House Hotel** stands in the centre of Grasmere village, on Red Bank Road, with the majestic peak of Silver Howe rising behind it and a breathtaking view across Grasmere Lake to the fore. This elegant hotel is set in two acres of beautiful gardens with a screened, heated outdoor swimming pool. Inside, the cosy bedrooms are all en-suite and excellently equipped, and downstairs the comfortable lounge offers a superb view of the Fairfield Horseshoe fell range. In the charming restaurant you can enjoy the imaginative table d'hote menu, which has won awards from both the RAC and the AA. The hotel also has the distinction of being entered in Ashley Courtenay's, which is renowned as the hallmark of good hotels.

Gold Rill Country House Hotel   Grasmere   05374 35486

If you are staying around Grasmere, but prefer somewhere a step away from the busy village, there are numerous hotels and bed & breakfast places nearby, from which you can get out to the fells easily, or in to explore more of Grasmere itself. Just a short walk from the village you will find **Forest Side**, a splendid Victorian mansion set in 40 acres of wooded and lawned grounds with outstanding views on all sides. This is one of Countrywide Holidays Association's finest houses. Established 100 years ago, the Association pioneered walking and special interest holidays, and today also provides excellent value accommodation for all holidaymakers. Forest Side has a residential licence and both the main house and the adjoining Coach House offer first class bed and breakfast accommodation. For those who prefer, the Coach House also has some excellent self-catering flats. With beautiful walks, panoramic views and the area's strong association with the Lakeland poets, Forest Side is an ideal holiday base. Accommodation can be booked directly with the house. For special interest and walking holidays, telephone 061 225 1000.

Forest Side   Grasmere   05394 35252

Just a little way outside Grasmere the Wordsworth story continues at **Rydal Mount**, where William, his sister and his wife lived from 1813 until 1850, when he died. This is a handsome house, overlooking Rydal Water, and it is still owned by descendants of the Wordsworth family, who have opened it to the public, as well as the gardens that William laid out himself. Among other possessions on display, the house contains the only portrait of Wordsworth's sister, Dorothy. From the Grasmere end of Rydal Water there are some lovely walks around the two lakes or to the summit of Loughrigg Fell, an easily manageable walk which rewards with breathtaking views of the lakes.

Lancrigg Country House Hotel Grasmere   05394 35317

Enjoying an enviable location about half a mile from Grasmere village, overlooking the tranquil scenery of Easedale, **Lancrigg Vegetarian Country House Hotel** offers you everything you could possibly want for that quiet break away from it all. Once a favourite haunt of

Wordsworth, Lancrigg was bought by his friend, Elizabeth Fletcher in 1839 and soon became a meeting place for Lakeland poets. Today it provides luxurious accommodation in individually styled guest rooms. A mouthwatering wholesome menu is enjoyed in elegant, candlelit surroundings to a backdrop of soothing classical music. With 30 acres of woodland gardens to explore, leading to spectacular views of the nearby fells, you may well end your stay at Lancrigg feeling you have had a taste of heaven! One of our colleagues is vegetarian and recommends both the food and the lovely setting of Lancrigg.

Bramriggs is another delightful country house enjoying a hilltop setting about one and a half miles outside Grasmere, with beautiful views over the valley. The garden borders on a footpath to Helvellyn and in the summer the air is heavy with the scent of azaleas. Run by Major and Mrs Fisher, Bramriggs is a non-smoking establishment which offers three comfortable and attractively furnished guest rooms. In the morning you can awake to the sound of a cockerel and feast on a breakfast of free range eggs and traditional Cumberland sausage, or a special vegetarian breakfast if you prefer. With the side garden leading down to the old pack horse trails, there is easy access to country walks in this beautiful area of the Lake District.

Bramriggs   Grasmere   05394 35360

From Grasmere, the A591 goes south to **Ambleside**, also a centre for extremely good walks, most notably into the high fells to the north of the town. Ambleside is a pretty town - look out for the **Old Bridge House**, a tiny cottage perched on a little packhorse bridge in the centre of the town, now a National Trust shop. In the 1850's this was the home of Mr and Mrs Rigg and their six children - the main room of this one-up, one-down house measures 13ft x 6ft!

Visitors to Ambleside will receive a warm welcome at **The Royal**

165

Oak situated on Main Street. Originally built in 1846, it was apparently Wordsworth's 'local' and had a brewery at the back of the pub. It has been run by Bill and Pat Cook for the past 20 years and is a charming pub with rustic tables outside where you can enjoy a drink in fine weather, and clematis cascading over the entrance porch. Inside you will find attractive beamed ceilings, and walls covered with photographs of ships, mementoes of Bill's years in the Merchant Navy. During the winter months you can make use of the pool table, and bar snacks are available all year round.

The Royal Oak   Ambleside   05394 33382

Situated just 3/4 of a mile from the centre of the delightful village of Ambleside, **Loughrigg Brow** is an impressive country house set in 39 acres of beautiful grounds on the side of Loughrigg Hill. Originally built in the 1860's for Canon Bell, the village Rector, Loughrigg Brow is now another of the thirteen houses nationwide owned by Countrywide Holidays Association, who also own Forest Side at Grasmere and Glaramara in Borrowdale. At Loughrigg Brow you will find very comfortable centrally heated accommodation and fine food, providing you with the ideal holiday base. The peaceful, elevated position of this welcoming house offers breathtaking views and superb walking country, and for the more serious hiker/climber, many major peaks are a short drive away. Accommodation is booked directly with Loughrigg Brow, and special interest and walking holidays can be arranged, as previously mentioned, by telephoning 061 225 1000.

A steep road climbs sharply out of the town centre, from the A591 Keswick - Windermere road up to the dramatic **Kirkstone Pass**, and over to Ullswater, making this a convenient position from which to explore the whole of the Lake District.

Loughrigg Brow   Ambleside   05394 32229

About 3/4 mile up this winding road out of Ambleside, known locally as The Struggle, you will find the delightful **Rowanfield Country House** snuggled into the hillside. The panorama of Lake Windermere and surrounding mountains will enthral. Run by Jane and Philip Butcher, this friendly non-smoking home from home offers many comforts. All rooms are individually and stylishly furnished with some lovely personal touches. Guest bedrooms have their own private bath/shower room, hot drinks facilities, colour TV and of course superb view. The house is warm and welcoming with an enticing guests lounge made all the more cosy in the cooler months with a blazing log fire. Each evening Philip creates a delicious meal. A top professional and international chef, the standard of food is far and above one's expectations of a small country house. Rowanfield makes an ideal base for walking or touring the area.

Rowanfield Country House   Ambleside   05394 33686

167

Continue to the top of Kirkstone Road and join the Kirkstone Pass, where you will find Britain's original mountain inn, the third highest pub in England. Built in 1496 as a refuge for travellers and road builders, The **Kirkstone Pass Inn** is now popular with walkers and skiers who call in to warm themselves with hot chocolate or mulled wine. The inn's original character is evident in the bar's low ceilings, oak beams and open log fires, and upstairs the comfortable guest rooms come complete with four poster beds and beautiful quilts. There is a variety of wholesome home-cooked food available, one of the favourites being Corned Beef and Leek Pie. All these factors combine to ensure an unforgettable experience for all who stay here.

Kirkstone Pass Inn   *Ambleside*   *05394 33624*

The Kirkstone Pass is so called because of a rock at the top which looks like a church steeple, and Kirk is still used in Scotland today as their word for 'church'.

Take the A593 a little way out of Ambleside, to **Elterwater** and **The Britannia Inn**, the very picture of a traditional country inn, lying next to the green of this pretty, unspoilt Cumbrian village. Outside in the summer months, guests can enjoy a drink or bar meal at one of the mass of garden tables on the Inn's terraced forecourt Inside there is a comfortable residents' lounge and dining room, with beams, an open log fire and antique furniture giving it a cosy, welcoming feel. The Britannia's bar is open all day throughout the year and serves traditional, cask-conditioned ales. There are tasty bar meals and snacks available every lunchtime and evening, as well as an afternoon menu of light snacks and cream teas to complete the service. Accommodation comprises nine double or twin-bedded rooms, six of which have en-suite shower and toilet. All the rooms have individually controlled central heating, colour TV, hot drinks facilities, hairdryer and telephone. Alternative accommodation, comprising one single, one twin, and two double rooms, one en-suite, is offered at Maple Tree Corner, the village shop immediately across from the Inn. Again excellent facilities are provided, and guests partake of a traditional English breakfast in the Britannia's dining room. The Britannia also has two holiday cottages available for weekly hire from March to October, for those who prefer self-catering accommodation. A very popular place, recommended.

The Britannia Inn   Elterwater   05394 37210

From the centre of Ambleside, follow the A591 south towards the town of **Windermere**, skirting the edge of Lake Windermere. This is a very pretty drive at any time of the year, along a tree-lined stretch of the lake which changes colour dramatically with each season.

The Sun Hotel   Troutbeck Bridge   05394 43274

Before you come into Windermere you will find **The Sun Hotel** at **Troutbeck Bridge**, a popular, traditional style country hotel, with beamed ceilings and dark wood furnishings. The bar and restaurant areas have been tastefully refurbished by the proprietors, David and Sonia Reid, offering attractive surroundings in which to sample the varied and reasonably priced food that is available. There is a good set menu and a wide selection of daily specials, including a vegetarian dish of the day. The accommodation comprises ten letting bedrooms, half with en-suite facilities, and three twin-bedded cottages to the rear of the Hotel have just been added to the property. Visitors can enjoy the Hotel's private access to a beach on Lake Windermere, with use of a boat and the provision of hampers on request, to complete an idyllic outing.

Quarry Garth Hotel   Troutbeck Bridge   09662 3761

Troutbeck Bridge also provides the picturesque setting for **Quarry Garth Country House Hotel**, an impressive period establishment where careful refurbishment has provided every modern comfort whilst retaining the original character of the building. The atmosphere here is one of friendly hospitality in luxurious surroundings, with beautifully decorated en-suite guest rooms providing every facility and having the added bonus of a lovely view and a welcoming hospitality tray on your arrival. The relaxing olde worlde ambience is enhanced by open log fires and original oak panelling throughout, whilst the elegant dining room provides the perfect setting for superb cuisine and wines which locals regularly travel some distance to enjoy. Set in beautiful grounds and surrounded by breathtaking scenery, this is a real haven for visitors seeking to "get away from it all".

Next to Troutbeck Bridge, at **Troutbeck**, it is worth going to visit **Town End**, built in about 1626 by a yeoman farmer called George Browne, and occupied by the Browne family until 1944. The house is now open to the public and contains a collection of the family's furniture, tools and artefacts over the generations.

Windermere is perhaps the Lake District's best known tourist centre.

The confusion of names between the town and the lake goes back to the days when the Kendal and Windermere Railway Company was opened in 1847. Its terminal station was at the village of Birthwaite - hardly a name to bring the tourists flocking in - so the railway company called their station Windermere, even though it is over a mile away from the lake. In the early days carriages and , in later years, buses linked the station with the landing stages in the village of Bowness on the shores of the lake.

Such was the popularity of the Lake District, even in Victorian times, that a town filled with hotels, boarding houses, comfortable villas and shops soon sprang up around the railway station. It spread rapidly down the hill towards the lake until Bowness and Birthwaite were linked together under the name of Windermere Town, the lake being given the unnecessary prefix, 'Lake' Windermere.

Windermere's railway line remains open as a single track branch - 'The Lakes Line' - now the only surviving British Rail line to run into the heart of the Lake District. Modern diesel railcars provide a busy shuttle service to and from the express services at Oxenholme. The rail journey via Kendal, Burneside and Staveley is a delight, and a very pleasant alternative to the crowded A591 road. Within a few yards of Windermere Station, just across the busy main road, there is a footpath that leads through the woods to one of the finest viewpoints in Lakeland, Orrest Head. It takes about an hour from the station to climb and descend the little hillock but there is no better introduction to this part of Cumbria.

Tucked down Phoenix Way, a quiet country lane in Windermere, you will find the appropriately named **Hideaway Hotel**. This lovely former Victorian mansion is set in its own well-tended gardens and has ample parking. Sympathetically converted, the hotel retains all its original charm, and provides every modern comfort in a warm, friendly environment. The 15 en-suite bedrooms are all tastefully furnished, and provide all the facilities you would expect. You can relax in the beautiful comfort of the guest lounge, or enjoy a drink in the cosy residents' bar before sampling excellent local and continental cuisine in the dining room. Guests at the hotel can also make use of the facilities at the local Parklands Country Club, of which the Hideaway is a member.

The Hideaway Hotel   Windermere   05394 43070

Conveniently situated on Ambleside Road, in the heart of Windermere, stands **Rockside Guest House**, an attractive traditional stone and slate built house. Close to the station and with its own off-road parking, Rockside offers excellent accommodation in a house full of character and charm. There are fifteen guest rooms ranging from single to family rooms, most with en-suite shower room and all with colour TV, radio, clock, telephone, electric blanket and central heating. With Windermere lake less than a mile away, and a tempting array of shops, restaurants and pubs in the village centre, Rockside makes an ideal base from which to explore this beautiful area of the Lake District.

Just a little way out of the town centre along the same road, a visit to **Brockhole National Park Centre** is one of the best ways to begin exploring. This Edwardian country house and estate has been carefully transformed into a visitor centre with displays and exhibitions of the Lake District National Park, its wildlife and customs. There is a restaurant and an excellent bookshop, but above all, miles of woodland and lakeside paths to explore, never more lovely than in the spring when the wild daffodils grow prolifically between the trees. Call into Windermere's Tourist Information Centre too, which is full of useful maps, guide books and information about all the local attractions.

Rockside Guest House   Windermere   05394 45353

Run by Tony and Sue Hoskers, **Oakthorpe Hotel** is a large Victorian listed building on High Street, in the heart of Windermere. Tastefully furnished, it offers nineteen guest rooms, half of which are en-suite, and all with colour TV. The tasty English breakfast is renowned as being one of the best in the area, and in the evening guests can partake of top class food in the adjoining Lamplighter Restaurant and Bar. Newly renovated to a high standard, the restaurant provides beautiful surroundings in which to sample the superb food prepared by Tony, who trained as a chef in Switzerland. Both he and Sue offer warm, friendly service and there is an information room with a wealth of literature to help visitors plan their stay.

Oakthorpe Hotel   Windermere   05394 43547

Turning by the Post Office in the centre of Windermere, Heatherbank

173

Guest House on Birch Street makes an ideal touring base for the Lake District and is a lovely place to return to at the end of a day's exploring. Originally built in 1898, this former Farrier's is run by friendly hosts Denise and Alan Potter and offers peace and quiet along with first class facilities. There are five attractively furnished en-suite guest rooms and every modern convenience is provided here, including satellite TV. Particularly noted for her excellent breakfasts, Denise is also happy to provide evening meals by arrangement, catering for vegetarian and special diets if required.

Heatherbank Guest House   Windermere   05394 46503

Visitors to the Lake District seeking bed and breakfast accommodation with that extra touch of luxury and class need look no further than **Fir Trees**, a charming Victorian guest house enjoying a quiet location on Lake Road, midway between the lakeside village of Bowness and Windermere. To give you an idea of what you can expect, Fir Trees has been featured in Ashley Courtenay's 1993 Guide to Highly Recommended Hotels, where it states, "In short, Fir Trees is undoubtedly one of the best bed and breakfast establishments in the area,...." Elegantly furnished, with beautiful antiques and fine prints enhancing the original character of the property, you feel as though you are in a first class hotel, but the friendly attentiveness of your hosts, Ira and Allene Fishman creates a welcoming, homely atmosphere. The spacious guest rooms are beautifully decorated, providing every modern amenity to ensure a relaxing stay. Awaking refreshed, the temptation is to linger in the comfort and peace of your surroundings, but the morning brings a treat well worth rousing yourself for. Heading downstairs, you will detect the delicious aroma of the full English breakfast, which is guaranteed to set you up for the day. Fir Trees is ideally situated, not only for Bowness and Windermere both of which are within easy walking distance, but also for the rest of the Lake District. Whatever your interests, walking, riding, sightseeing or simply absorbing the breathtaking beauty of the Lakeland countryside, there is something to suit everyone and with the luxurious comfort of Fir Trees to return to, your stay here is complete.

Fir Trees   Windermere   05394 42272

Also on Lake Road, **Sandown-Kempton Guest House** is a very attractive, modern establishment run by friendly hosts, Irene and George Eastwood.   Set in lovely grounds with plenty of off-road parking, this large house is immaculate and provides very spacious and beautifully decorated accommodation in seven letting rooms, with all the modern comforts one comes to expect. You can spend your evenings relaxing in the cosy guest lounge and awake refreshed in the morning to enjoy a superb breakfast in the bright, airy breakfast room. The beautiful surroundings and experienced, attentive hosts ensure Sandown is the sort of place you will return to time and again.

Sandown-Kempton Guest House   Windermere 05394 45275

175

Merewood Country House Hotel, at Ecclerigg, is an impressive establishment standing in 20 acres of landscaped woodland gardens, overlooking Lake Windermere. Here the warm welcome is matched by the comfort and luxury of the sumptuous surroundings. The Conservatory Bar is evocative of the Edwardian era, with its mahogany panelling, beautiful mosaic floor and red chesterfield sofas. In the Billiard Room Restaurant with its elegant yew tables, you can enjoy a first class menu of English and French cuisine, including a creative range of vegetarian dishes all accompanied by an extensive international wine list. Upstairs equal thought and care has gone into the individually decorated bedrooms. All are very spacious, beautifully furnished and with the top class facilities you would expect. It therefore comes as no surprise to learn that Merewood has received the five crown, highly commended award, one of the English Tourist Board's highest accolades. Having stayed here recently, we think it is ideal for a spoil yourself weekend. They do a very good dinner, bed and breakfast; recommended.

Merewood Country Hotel   Windermere   05394 46484

Bowness is an attractive, albeit busy, town, right on the edge of the lake, and it is from here that most of the lake cruises operate. More than just England's largest lake, Windermere is actually a public highway or, more correctly, waterway. This ten-mile stretch of water, with its thickly wooded banks and scattered islands, has been used since Roman times as a means of transport. Roman Legionnaires used it for carrying stone to their fort at 'Galava', near present-day Ambleside, at the head of the lake. The monks of Furness Abbey fished for pike and char - a rare form of trout and a local delicacy. When the railway came, handsome paddle-steamers linked Bowness with Ambleside and **Lakeside** at the southern end of the lake where the Railway Company had a station and an hotel. The hotel and station survive, as does the railway as far as the village of **Haverth-**

waite. It is operated, during the summer months, by the Lakeside and Haverthwaite Steam Railway Company. There are few nicer ways to spend a summer day in the Lake District than taking one of the handsome, vintage boats of the Windermere Iron Steamboat Company from Ambleside or Bowness Pier down to Lakeside for a trip on the three-mile steam railway through the woods.

Less than a mile from Lakeside, near the hamlet of **Finsthwaite**, is **Stott Park Bobbin Mill**, an early Victorian mill which has been beautifully restored as a working industrial monument and Visitor Centre, with a water-powered turbine and a steam-driven mill engine.

Only a short way from **Newby Bridge**, at the foot of Windermere, on the opposite shore from Lakeside, is Fell Foot Country Park, an area alongside the lake with lovely views, a playground and picnic areas.

Bowness is not all crowds and boats. Away from the marinas and the car parks is the old village, where St Martin's Church is of particular interest. It has a magnificent East Window filled with 14th and 15th century glass and an unusual 300-year old wooden carved figure of St Martin, sharing his cloak with a beggar.

Attractions that are well worth visiting in Bowness include the **Windermere Steam Boat Museum**, on the lake shore north of Bowness, with a unique collection of Victorian and Edwardian steam launches, including the 'S.L. Dolly', the oldest mechanically powered boat in the world. Also **The Old Laundry Visitor Centre**, home of the World of Beatrix Potter, an excellent walk-round centre with beautifully made tableaux of the Beatrix Potter characters and a handy coffee shop downstairs. The Old Laundry is also a centre for exhibitions, theatre and holiday activities (telephone 05394 88444).

Gilpin Lodge Hotel   Windermere   05394 88818

Gilpin Lodge, on Crook Road, is a magnificent country house hotel and restaurant set in 20 acres of gardens, woodland and moors. A converted country house, it is a family run business where attention to detail is the key. The beautifully furnished accommodation has an air of relaxed sophistication, with elegant antique furniture, richly coloured fabrics and freshly cut flowers in all the rooms. The bedrooms are all individual in style and exceptionally well equipped, some with four poster and whirlpool bath. The highlight of each day however is the excellent five course dinner served in the elegant dining room where the menu is varied and imaginative and accompanied by an extensive, quality wine list. All these factors have earned Gilpin Lodge a 4-crown, Highly Commended rating by the English Tourist Board. Nearby is the car ferry that links Bowness with Sawrey, on the opposite side of the lake, which is an attraction in itself, and an important form of transport - without it, travellers would have a long drive around the lake along winding lanes, to reach the villages of Hawkshead, Sawrey, Satterthwaite and Coniston. It's a very frequent service and approximate waiting times are posted on the approach roads.

Just south of Bowness, at the appropriately-named Ferry View on the A5074 road to Lyth Valley, stands **Brooklands**, a delightful guest house run by Pauline and Barry Holland. Having previously run a popular guest house in Blackpool, Barry and Pauline are experienced and friendly hosts who will soon have you relaxing in the comfort of their charming home. There are six spacious and attractively decorated en-suite guest rooms ranging from single to family size, all centrally heated and well-equipped. This lovely Victorian house boasts wonderful views of Windermere Lake and the surrounding fells, which can be seen to full advantage from the window of the small sitting area situated on the top floor of the house.

Brooklands   Bowness-on-Windermere   05394 42344

The village of **Underbarrow** lies in a beautiful area of rolling hills about three or four miles between Bowness and Kendal. In this area steeped in history and lying on the old Woolpack route, you will find the

Underbarrow Punchbowl, a traditional English pub dating back to the 1500's. Run by former merchant navy seaman, David Howarth, the Punchbowl is renowned for plentiful, reasonably priced bar food which is available throughout the day. It is also noted for the traditional Draught Bass ales which are served, and was rated by the Daily Telegraph as offering the best pint in the North West. Adjoining the pub, David has established a caravan park where he lets caravans by the week. This area to the east of Lake Windermere is relatively little known, but it is delightful to explore, dotted with little hamlets, good country pubs and beautiful views across the rolling, hilly landscape.

Underbarrow Punchbowl   Underbarrow   05395 68234

Staveley, now by-passed, is a village of great charm through which runs a stream crossed by footbridges. It lies at the foot of the little Kentmere Valley, a quiet cul-de-sac leading to the hamlet of **Kentmere** itself. As its name implies, part of this valley was once a lake, drained to provide precious bottom pasture land. A large mill-pond remains to provide a head of water on the River Kent for use at a paper mill. This is a beautiful valley to explore on foot - a public path goes up the western side of the valley past Kentmere Hall, a fortified pele tower, now a farmhouse. From the hamlet itself, where an ancient packhorse track climbs over Garburn Pass to Troutbeck and Windermere, there is a spectacular walk, easily done by leaving a car at Windermere and using the train to return to Staveley.

The River Kent, which runs down into Kendal from Staveley via Burneside, carries the Dales Way from Yorkshire into the Lake District along its banks, an attractive stretch of riverside path, richly varied in character from mill-dam to rapids, and a haven for wildlife. Just south of Burneside, the River Sprint, a tributary, meets the Kent. The Sprint has its own, remarkably beautiful Longsleddale Valley which curves past

Garnett Bridge deep into the high fell country. A bridle path climbs from the head of the valley into Kentmere, another spectacularly beautiful walk.

Equally little known, yet so very close to Windermere, is the country-side of the Winster Valley, south of Staveley, and the Lyth Valley, which the main A5074 from Bowness, follows south to Levens. A network of narrow lanes links tiny hamlets like **Winster**, **Bowland Bridge** and Underbarrow, across this area of low, spikey hills, not as spectacular as the central fells, but full of character and a special charm. There are some excellent pubs here too, off the beaten track, and well worth seeking out, especially the **Mason's Arms** at Strawberry Bank, which is listed in the Guiness Book of Records for selling the greatest number of different beers - over one hundred, including their own Damson beer, brewed on the premises. The Lyth Valley is also famous for its damson blosson in the Spring.

Lightwood   Cartmel Fell   05395 31454

Visitors to **Lightwood**, a delightful 17th century farmhouse near Bowland Bridge, in Cartmel Fell, will receive a warm welcome from hosts Evelyn and Fideo Cervetti. This lovely home has been in Evelyn's family since 1945 and enjoys an idyllic location just 2 miles from the southern end of Lake Windermere. You can relax in the two acres of beautiful gardens, whilst inside you will find a cosy atmosphere with the oak beams and inglenook fireplaces retaining Lightwood's original charm. The accommodation comprises 9 bedrooms, six of which are en-suite, and all beautifully furnished in keeping with the character of this lovely old farmhouse. As well as providing a wholesome breakfast, Evelyn and Fideo make your stay complete by offering a four-course dinner, prepared using fresh homegrown produce.

180

The countryside west of Lake Windermere is an area of low, thickly wooded hills, most easily reached by taking the car ferry from Bowness to **Far Sawrey**. Once across, the road takes you through **Near Sawrey**, a little village best known for another Lakeland celebrated literary figure, Beatrix Potter, whose home, Hill Top, is now a National Trust property and a museum.

Continue along this road to **Hawkshead**, at the head of Esthwaite Water. The village has changed little since William Wordsworth, at the age of eight, attended the Grammar School here, and it is all the better preserved since visitors are obliged to leave their cars outside the village centre and walk through it on foot. Next to the car park is the National Park Information Centre, a good starting point for exploring Hawkshead. A nice way to go into the village is past the Grammar School and through the churchyard. The 15th century church dominates Hawkshead from its high position, and is worth a look inside for its series of painted murals which date from 1680.

Hawkshead Grammar School

The footpath brings you out in the market square, enclosed by 17th and 18th century shops and cottages. Overlooking the square of this Elizabethan village stands **The Kings Arms Hotel**, an ancient Lakeland Inn full of character, with log fires for those chilly evenings. Rosalie Johnson the proprietor, offers a warm welcome to all her guests and looks after them very well. She will happily provide packed lunches for those day-long excursions, and in the evening you can choose from an excellent range of home-cooked dishes. With an extensive wine list to accompany your meal plus a choice of four real ales and wide selection of malt and Irish whiskeys at the bar, your evening is complete. Finally you can retire to one of the nine well-equipped guest rooms, or make use of the self-catering accommodation in nearby Fern Cottage which sleeps four.

The Kings Arms Hotel   Hawkshead   05394 36372

The National Trust now owns some of the buildings in Hawkshead, including 'Bend or Bump', which was formerly a house and shop, and features in Beatrix Potter's "The Pie and the Patty Pan", and the former solicitor's office of William Heelis, who was Beatrix Potter's husband. This building is now the Beatrix Potter Gallery.

Hawkshead Town Trail takes you to these places, and to the cottage of Anne Tyson, where Wordsworth lodged as a student.

Ivy House Hotel   Hawkshead   05394 36204

Just outside the centre of Hawkshead, **Ivy House Hotel** is a Grade II listed Georgian house, full of character and charm, with a feature spiral staircase enticing you upstairs to the spacious and attractively decorated en-suite guest rooms. Six rooms are in the main house and five in Mere Lodge, just across the drive. Children are welcome, with two family rooms plus high chairs and cots available. The table licence enables you to complement the tasty dinner menu with a suitable wine, whilst the cosy lounge is the perfect place to relax in front of a log fire.

Some lovely walks lead from Hawkshead to Roger Ground and Esthwaite and to the nearby hamlet of Colthouse, a group of farmsteads and cottages with a Quaker Meeting House built in 1688.

Grizedale

One of the most interesting places to visit from Hawkshead is **Grizedale**, famous for its Theatre and Sculpture. In the forest more than 100 sculptures have been commissioned over the last fifteen years, all made from natural materials found in the forest, and by some of Britain's best known contemporary artists, including the sculptor Andy Goldsworthy, as well as artists from all over the world. The great beauty of these sculptures is their understated presence - here you won't find any signposts pointing to the next exhibit, you are left entirely to your own devices to explore the wonders of this forest, with the help of a printed guide, either on foot or on mountain bike, which can be hired at the Visitor Centre.

The **Theatre-in-the-Forest** has an excellent programme throughout the year of musical and theatrical events of the highest quality, and the Visitor Centre now includes an art gallery and workshop which is also open to the public, where the artists in residence will happily take a break from their work to describe their experiences of living and working in this unique environment. For details of "What's On" at the theatre, telephone 0229 860291.

The **Grizedale Lodge Hotel**, in the heart of this magnificent forest, is very much a 'hidden place' that is well worth seeking out. Your friendly hosts, Jack and Margaret Lamb have nine beautifully furnished en-suite guest rooms, all equipped to the highest standard for complete comfort. Margaret, an authority on Cumbrian food, has had her own cookery series on Border Television, and her skill is self-evident in the mouthwatering dinner menu which includes local venison, trout, salmon and lamb dishes. After dinner, the Lounge Bar is the perfect place to relax, with French doors leading to a balcony with patio furniture for those fine summer evenings. With breathtaking beauty all around and superb accommodation and service, you really could not want for more.

Grizedale Lodge Hotel   Hawkshead   05394 36532

A short distance further South, the Lakeland village of **Satterthwaite** nestles in the beautiful countryside of the Grizedale valley, between Coniston Water and Windermere Lake. It is in this lovely setting that visitors will find **Pepper House**, a top class, fully licensed guest house. Run by Yvonne Smith, this charming Elizabethen farmhouse is full of character with oak cruck beams and thick stone walls. The bedrooms are all en-suite with excellent facilities, including one ground floor room adapted for wheelchair users. The real feather in Yvonne's cap is the mouthwatering, value for money, home-cooked meals she prepares. Using traditional British recipes and some of her own creation, Yvonne caters to all tastes and keeps mealtimes flexible for guests' convenience.

Pepper House   Satterthwaite   0229 860206

One of the most famous of all Lakeland valleys is of course, **Langdale** - steep, flat-bottomed and surrounded by towering peaks. It is spectacularly beautiful, particularly the famous Langdale Pike at the head of the valley above Dungeon Ghyll, and is a mecca for hillwalkers and climbers. Like so much of the Lake District this is an area best enjoyed on foot. There are easy paths along the valley floor all the way from Elterwater and Chapel Stile to Stickle Tarn or Blea Tarn at the head of the valley. Further walks, for the more experienced, lead to the summit of England's highest mountain, Scafell Pike, to Great Gable and other challenging peaks.

Strictly speaking, the valley most people refer to as Langdale is Great Langdale; the parallel valley is Little Langdale. A steep and narrow moorland road, Side Gate, links the two. At the head of Little Langdale is the Wrynose Pass, a murderously-steep road, not for the faint-hearted, over to the head of the Duddon Valley and the even steeper Hardknott Pass to **Eskdale**.

The Duddon Valley, or Dunnerdale, which runs from **Wrynose Bottom** to **Duddon Sands**, is a particularly lovely, less well-known part of Lakeland. Richly wooded yet squeezed between high mountains, it has no major tourist attractions, just a landscape of rare quality. Immediately south of the little car park by Hinning House is the famous Birk's Bridge, an ancient pack-horse bridge in a perfect setting.

Tucked away in the quiet little hamlet of **Seathwaite** in the Duddon Valley is the **Newfield Inn**, a charming, traditional inn run by two brothers, Andy and Chris Burgess. Here they serve three kinds of Theakston ales, including the very strong "Old Peculiar". The wholesome bar meals are excellent value and the portions are very generous,

Birk's Bridge, Dunnerdale

with favourites being the steaks, the large gammon, and the very special steak pies. Adjacent to the inn Andy and Chris have two self catering flats which can sleep up to six people comfortably. This peaceful location in a totally unspoilt area of the Lake District is a walker's paradise, with ready access to Coniston Fell, The Furness Way and the Forestry Commission walks.

The Newfield Inn   Seathwaite   0229 716208

The road switchbacks down the valley through Seathwaite, which has a delightful church, to the village of **Ulpha**, the name meaning 'Wolf Hill'. There are some magnificent walks within and from this valley across the fells towards Ravenglass, Coniston or Torver.

Coniston Water is one of the more famous lakes yet one which is considerably less crowded than many of the others. Coniston Water is a gentler lake than Windermere, and the little town at its head, which shares its name, was once an important copper-mining centre. It is widely known for the beautiful decorative green slate, quarried locally, which is used on so many public buildings. You can still follow tracks from the centre of Coniston into the old copper-workings, long since closed. These provide part of the ascent of the Old Man of Coniston, 2631ft above sea level and a fine viewpoint. Coniston is a pleasant, unpretentious little town with a small museum in memory of John Ruskin who lived at nearby Brantwood.

Coniston Water, because of its relative calmness, was used for water-speed record attempts. It has seen its share of triumph and tragedy in the careers of Malcolm Campbell and his son, Donald, who perished on the lake in an attempt to break the world record in 1967. A memorial to him is in the centre of Coniston village.

Happier association lies with memories of the author Arthur Ransome who used Coniston as a setting for his series of children's novels. Peel Island, at the south end of the lake, is the 'Wildcat Island' of the books.

But it is John Ruskin, the great art-historian, artist, moralist and critic who has perhaps the strongest links with Coniston. A narrow road, beautiful but not easy to drive along, will take you to **Brantwood** around the far side of the Lake. The nicest way of getting there, however, is to take the superbly restored National Trust Steam Launch Gondola which cuts silently across the water as you enjoy the opulent luxury of its red velvet seats. Brantwood is more than just a shrine to Ruskin, the man who probably did more to create an awareness of the fine arts and architecture in Britain than any other. It is a magnificent country estate with a series of trails leading to superb view-points across Coniston Water to the surrounding hills. If you stand in Ruskin's study and share that incomparable view of the lake, you begin to understand just something of what motivated his genius. There is also a large car park and an excellent tearoom here within the old stables called 'Jumping Jenny', named after John Ruskin's boat.

The Old Rectory Hotel   Torver   05394 41353

Just a few miles south of Coniston, in the village of **Torver** you will find a delightful place to stay at **The Old Rectory Country House Hotel**. Set in three acres of lovely wooded grounds, this beautifully refurbished Victorian house boasts magnificent views of the surrounding National Trust Farmland. Your welcoming hosts Paul and Caroline Fletcher have developed The Old Rectory into a truly first class establishment. The attractively decorated en-suite guest rooms provide spacious and well-equipped accommodation, whilst the dining room offers beautiful views from the large picture windows and provides a charming setting in which to enjoy the imaginative and mouthwatering menus. All these factors combine to ensure that your stay here will be a memorable one.

There are some lovely walks around Torver, for instance across the fells into one of the Lake District's most tranquil 'hidden places', the Duddon Valley.

CHAPTER SEVEN

Furness

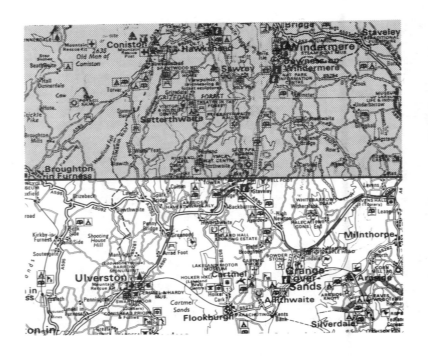

Kirkstile Inn and Church, Loweswater.

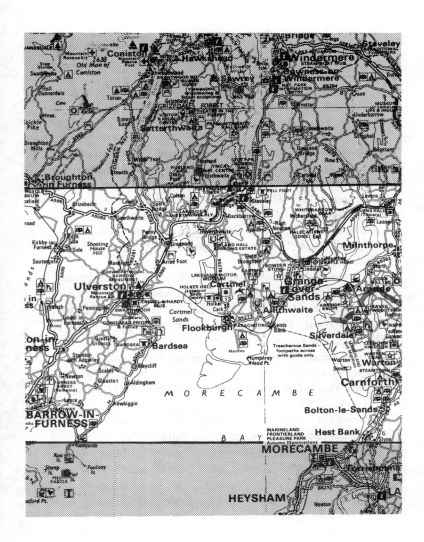

CHAPTER SEVEN

Index

Cartmel

Furness

Near Carnforth

CHAPTER SEVEN

Furness

Furness lies between the lakes and mountains of Cumbria and the great sandy estuaries of Morecambe Bay. It is an area of gentle moorland, craggy headlands, scattered woodlands and vast expanses of sand. Once the stronghold of the Cistercian monks, their influence is still felt in the buildings and in the fabric of the landscape. It is well worth taking time to explore this part of Cumbria, both for the variety and distinctiveness of its countryside and its rich, exciting past.

Lying in a narrow valley on the part of Furness which extends deep into Morecambe Bay, is the ancient town of **Dalton**. It is difficult to imagine that this was once the leading town of Furness and an important centre for administration and justice. The 14th-century pele tower, Dalton Castle, stands almost hidden by surrounding buildings. It was built around 1330-36 to provide a place of refuge for the monks of Furness Abbey against Scottish raiders. Over the centuries, in its twin role as both prison and court, it has been substantially altered internally, although it still retains most of its original external features. It is now owned by the National Trust and there is a small museum with an interesting display of 16th- and 17th-century armour.

Dalton became established as a market-town in the 13th century when the Cistercians began to hold fairs and markets in the town. Before the Dissolution of the Monasteries, it was the Abbot who held court and administered justice. Indeed, Dalton's decline coincided with the decline of the monks and the growing importance of Ulverston and Greenodd as ports.

The red sandstone Church of St Mary was designed by the celebrated Victorian architects Paley and Austin. In the graveyard lies George Romney (1734-1804), the famous portrait painter, who was born in the town. Spend some time looking around the many fascinating facades in and around Market Place, such as the unique, cast-iron shop front at No 51, Market Street. In the Market Place itself is an elegant, Victorian drinking fountain, with fluted columns supporting a dome of open iron-work above the pedestal fountain. Nearby, stands the market cross and slabs of stone that were used for fish-drying in the 19th century.

On the northern outskirts of Dalton is the **Clarence House Country Hotel and Restaurant**, an exceptional establishment situated on the western side of the A595 Broughton-in-Furness road at Skelgate, half-a-mile from the centre of Dalton. Built in 1880 for a local mine manager, the present owners, Tom and Pauline Barber, bought this impressive residence in 1975 as their private family home. They had, however, shared a lifelong ambition of owning and running a restaurant and hotel and set in motion a demanding programme of building renovation and re-furbishment. Two-and-a-half years later, their ambition began to be realised when they opened the restaurant and a single bed and breakfast room for the first time. Today, Clarence House boasts fifteen luxurious guest bedrooms all of which are individually decorated and equipped with en suite facilities, colour televisions, telephones and beverage making facilities. Most also have wonderful views over the beautifully-kept three-acre garden to the lovely wooded valley beyond. Some of the more recently converted rooms are situated in the charming old coach houses and artisans' cottages which stand adjacent to the main building. The Clarence House Restaurant has a reputation for serving some of the best food in the area. Its first-class menu is changed regularly and includes the finest English and continental dishes including game in season. On weekday evenings, a top quality carvery is offered in addition to the normal menu. Residents enjoy their meal in the elegant surroundings of the dining room which leads out onto a delightful slate-flagged patio. The special quality of Clarence House is that on one hand it is very stylishly decorated, yet on the other it retains the relaxed welcoming atmosphere of a family country home, making this a truly outstanding place to stay when visiting this attractive but lesser-known part of Cumbria.

Clarence House   Dalton-in-Furness   0229 62508

To the south of Dalton is **Furness Abbey**, a magnificent ruin of eroded red sandstone set in fine parkland, the focal point of South Cumbria's monastic heritage. You can still see the canopied seats in the presbytery and the graceful arches overlooking the cloister, testaments to the Abbey's former wealth and influence.

Furness Abbey stands in the **Vale of Deadly Nightshade**, a shallow valley of sandstone cliffs and rich pastureland. The Abbey itself was established in 1123 at Tulketh, near Preston, by Stephen, Count of Blois and King of England. Four years later it was moved to its present site and, after twenty years, became absorbed into the Cistercian Order. Despite its remoteness, the Abbey flourished with the monks establishing themselves as guides across the treacherous sands of Morecambe Bay. Rich endowments of land, which included holdings in Yorkshire and Ireland, led to the development of trade in products such as wool, iron and charcoal. It became the second wealthiest monastery in Britain after Fountains Abbey in Yorkshire.

After Dissolution in 1537 it became part of Thomas Cromwell's

Furness Abbey

estate, and was allowed to decay into a picturesque and romantic ruin. It is now owned by English Heritage who have a small Interpretative Centre nearby detailing its history.

Furness Abbey lies within walking distance of **Barrow**, another Cumbrian contrast. Barrow is a 19th-century industrial town with long, narrow streets of terraced houses around a busy centre. But, despite its industrial past, it has features of interest. Like many such towns in the last century, it grew up around a railway, built to transport locally-produced haematite (iron-ore), slate and limestone to a new deep-water port. Its original population was 200 but, by 1874, this had increased to over 35,000. However, it was steel production and ship-building that led to the town's real prosperity. James Ramsden established the first Barrow Iron Ship Company in 1870, taking advantage of local steel-production skills. In 1896 the firm was acquired by Vickers and for a number of years was the largest armaments works in the world.

You must still cross from Barrow Docks to Walney Island by a bridge which joins the ten-mile long island to the peninsular. **Walney Island**, reputedly the windiest lowland site in Britain is well worth visiting. It contains two particularly important Nature Reserves.

North Walney National Nature Reserve has an area for the preservation of the Natterjack toad, Britain's rarest amphibian. Over 130 species of birds have been recorded here, with more than twenty nesting species. Its 350 acres exhibit a great variety of habitats including sand-dunes, heath, salt-marsh, sandy beaches, shingle and scrub. As well as having several species of orchid, it has the richest shingle-beach flora in the UK. North Walney's wildlife is matched by it rich prehistoric past with important archaeological sites from Mesolithic, Neolithic, Bronze and Iron Age times.

South Walney Nature Reserve, along the island's long foot, only reached by path, has the largest nesting ground of Herring Gulls and Lesser Black-backed Gulls in Europe. It is also the most southerly breeding point of such species as Oyster Catcher, Tern and Ringed Plover. It serves as a stop-over for many migratory birds and the Reserve is of considerable ecological interest with mudflats, sandy beaches, rough pasture, freshwater and brackish pools. For the visitor there are trails to follow and an observation building near the entrance. The southern tip of Walney Point is dominated by a 70-ft lighthouse which was built in 1790 and originally provided light with an oil lamp. From Haws Point, there is a lovely view of Piel Island and its imposing Keep.

Piel Island is reached by ferry from Roa Island which is joined to the peninsular by a causeway. Piel Island was probably visited by the Celts and later by the Romans, but its first recorded name is Scandinavian

'Fotheray', from Old Norse meaning 'fodder island'. In 1127 the island was given to the Savignac Monks by King Stephen as part of their original land-grant for an Abbey. After the Savignacs merged with the Cistercians in the middle of the 12th century, Furness Abbey began to use the island as a warehouse and storage area, being both near to the Abbey and a safe harbour.

The motte-and-bailey castle on the island, built in the early part of the 14th century, was the largest of its kind in the north-west. It was intended to be used as a fortified warehouse protected against attacks from pirates and sea-raiders. However, in later years it also proved to be a useful defence against the King's Customs men and a prosperous trade in smuggling began.

Piel Castle

One of the most exciting events in Piel's history occurred on June 4th, 1487 when Lambert Simnel, a merchant's son, landed on the island. Simnel had claimed he was the Earl of Warwick (one of the Princes in the Tower said to have been murdered by Richard III) and therefore the rightful King of England. With an army of German and Irish mercenaries, Simnel set out across Furness to march to London. However, when he arrived in London it was as the prisoner of Henry VII, having been defeated by the King's forces at the Battle of Stoke.

Lambert Simnel's name lives on in Piel, where the landlord of the Ship Inn is traditionally known as 'King', after Simnel's claim to the title. In the Ship Inn is an old oaken chair and anyone who sits on it becomes a 'Knight of Piel'. The knighthood ceremony must be performed either by the 'King' or another 'Knight'. Following this the new 'Knight' is required to buy everyone a drink! A 'Knight' must be a moderate smoker, an ardent lover of the opposite sex and of good character. One of the rights of the 'Knight', if he is ship-wrecked on Piel, is that he may go to the inn and demand free lodgings and as much as he can eat and drink! When the tide is out there is the opportunity to walk to the Ship Inn on Piel Island for a drink - or several if you are marooned!

This part of Furness has many small hamlets and villages, such as Leece, Baycliff, Slaith and Gleaston. Each has its own identity and all can be reached from the beautiful Furness coast road, the A5087. **Gleaston Water Mill** is a renovated corn mill, which has been lovingly restored by its present owners. The mill contains working machinery and is now a centre of local crafts and country cooking, an extremely handy place for a well-earned rest. It is well worth paying a visit to the man in **The Leather Shop** who makes superb hand-painted leather belts. It is claimed that **Aldingham**, along the coast road, was once washed away by a tidal wave, but no one is quite sure of the truth of this story. However, do visit the **Church of St Cuthbert**, said to be one of the many places where the monks of Jarrow rested the Saint's body in their flight from the Danes. Inside the Church there is a charming statue of St Cuthbert with his otters, which was presented by Durham Cathedral. Parts of the Church date from the 12th century and there are some interesting old pieces of sculpture in the north aisle. Notice the crooked chancel arch, a feature occasionally found in old churches, meant to represent the body of Christ with his head leaning to one side. There is a hagioscope (window) in the wall to allow parishioners sitting in the south aisle to view the altar.

The ancient Church of St Mary and St Michael in **Great Urswick**, to the north west, also has a hagioscope. However, the great joy of this church is its unusual and lively woodcarvings by the Chipping Camden Guild of Carvers. Of particular note is the figure of a pilgrim, to the left of the chancel arch, and the small carvings in the choir-stall of winged children playing musical instruments. Look out for the three-decker pulpit with its scallop-shaped sounding board and the 9th-century wooden cross with a runic inscription. A rush-bearing ceremony is held in the church every September.

The road from Great Urswick leads on to **Birkrigg Common**, a lovely area of open land with a Bronze Age circle and superb views of the Bay.

At Sunbrick, on the edge of the Common, in the churchyard, is the unmarked grave of Margaret Fell who married George Fox, one of the founders of the Quaker movement.

Drop down to **Bardsea**, which stands on a lovely green knoll above the sea. Bardsea has an unhurried air about it and is an excellent base for short walks along the coast, either from its Country Park, along way-marked nature trails, or through its woodland.

Further along the coast is **Conishead Priory**, once the site of a leper colony, established by the Augustinian canons in the 12th century. In later years the monks used to act as guides across the dangerous Cartmel Sands which formed the only direct road to Lancaster. After Dissolution in 1539, a fine private house was built on the site and the Estuary Guide service was continued by the Duchy of Lancaster. In 1821, a Colonel Braddyll demolished the earlier house and built the present ornate Gothic mansion. He was also responsible for the atmospheric ruined folly on Chapel Island, clearly visible in the centre of the Levens Estuary. Conishead Priory later became a rest-home for Durham miners but is now owned by the Tibet Buddhist Manjushri Institute. The Institute is gradu-ally restoring the house and warmly welcomes visitors for tours of the house, or to follow a delighful woodland trail.

Ulverston is a fine market town in the centre of Furness, with old buildings and a labyrinth of cobbled streets and alleyways to explore. The town dates from the 12th century when Stephen, Earl of Boulogne and King of England, owned the Manor. In 1280 the town was granted a charter to hold a market and every Thursday and Saturday it bustles with activity as livestock are brought for sale and street-traders set up their stalls. Each September the charter is celebrated with events taking place daily for a two-week festival, culminating in a lantern procession, when the children of Ulverston make their own lanterns and parade through the streets at dusk.

The railway station, on what is now the Furness Line, was once the junction for the branch to Lakeside, and is an example of early Victorian railway architecture.

In the heart of Ulverston, on Church Walk, you will find an elegant 18th century former gentleman's residence, **Church Walk House**. This well cared for establishment has been lovingly restored to provide first class accommodation. The guest rooms have beautiful period furnish-ings and there is also a comfortable guest lounge. Your host Martin Chadderton is a trained chef and as well as serving a variety of tasty breakfast dishes, he will happily prepare a mouthwatering evening meal if required. This charming house had quite a prestigious start to its life as a guest house, when David Waddington (former Home Secretary),

Ludovic Kennedy and Jonathan Dimbleby all stayed here during filming for 'Any Questions'.

Church Walk House   *Ulverston*   *0229 52211*

The oldest building in Ulverston is the Church of St Mary which, in part, dates from AD1111. It was restoresd and rebuilt in the 1860's and a chancel added in 1903-4. The church is particularly noted for its splendid Norman door and some magnificent stained glass, including a window based on a design by the painter Sir Joshua Reynolds. The original steeple was destroyed in a storm in 1540 and the present tower dates from the reign of Elizabeth I.

Ulverston's most famous son is Stan Laurel, of Laurel and Hardy fame, who was born here in 1890. His real name was Arthur Stanley Jefferson and he spent his first fifteen years in a small terraced house, No. 3 Argyll Street. It now has a plaque commemorating him and a local pub has been renamed 'The Stan Laurel'.Nearby, at Upper Brook Street, is the Laurel and Hardy Museum, crammed with photographs and relics of the comedian and his Hollywood partner, Oliver Hardy.

On the outskirts of Ulverston is **Swarthmoor**, a small collection of white-washed cottages and a 16th century hall. Swarthmoor Hall stands in a well-kept garden and, although a cement rendering disguises its antiquity, the mullioned windows and leaded panes give a clue to its age. It was built around 1586 by George Fell, a wealthy land-owner and it was his son, Judge Thomas Fell, who was to marry Margaret Askew. In 1652 Margaret Fell heard George Fox preach and became convinced of 'The Truth'.However, many were suspicious of Fox's beliefs and he was to suffer rough treatment and persecution. Margaret was able to persuade her husband to use his position to give Fox protection and shelter, and the Hall became the first settled centre of the Quaker sect, the place where missionaries were organised. A library was started with both Quaker and anti-Quaker literature. Judge Fell died in 1658 and eleven years later Margaret married George Fox. The Hall is now open in the summer months and gives a fascinating insight into the history of the early Quakers.

The main coastal road winds round the top end of the Duddon Estuary to the village of **Broughton-in-Furness**, another delightful part of West Cumbria which deserves to be better known. This charming little market town, built on the side of a hill above the Duddon Valley, is filled with handsome 18th-century houses. The Market Hall still has its original 1766 clock, and the Market Square, from where the Market Charter is still proclaimed annually, has stone-slabbed stalls. Jack Hadwin's Motor Cycle Collection, in the Old Town Hall, boasts fifty machines dating from between 1899 to 1959 as well as items from the early days of motoring.

Cobblers Cottage   Broughton-in-Furness   0229 716413

In Griffin Street, a short distance from Broughton-in-Furness' historic Georgian square, is the delightful and reasonably priced small guesthouse and craft shop which is run by Susan and John Fletcher. Dating from 1672 and now Grade II listed, **Cobblers Cottage** retains a cosy traditional atmosphere with oak-beamed ceilings, a grandfather clock, a large open fireplace and a magnificent Georgian bow window. The bedrooms are spacious and furnished with washbasins, hot drinks' facilities and old pine furniture. As well as delicious English breakfasts, four-course dinners are available if required. The adjacent building houses the charming **Broughton Craft Shop**. Here, a wide range of quality crafts is stocked, many made by local Cumbrian craftspeople including slate jewellery handmade by the owners.

Broughton is an ideal base from which to explore the Duddon Valley and the relatively little-known fell-country all around, as well as the coast and northern Furness. And there are many surprises. About two miles west of Duddon Bridge, high up on Swinside Fell, and only reached by footpath, is Swinside Stone Circle, sometimes known as 'Sunkenkirk'. This prehistoric monument could be 3500 years old, and was built for a purpose that can only be guessed at.

Visitors to Broughton-in-Furness will discover more than just first class accommodation at **Eccle Riggs Manor**, on Foxfield Road. It stands in 30 acres of beautifully kept gardens with its own private par three golf course, and boasts fabulous views towards the distant mountains. Tastefully modernised, it offers all essential comforts, still retaining original features such as the glorious stained glass window over the main staircase, depicting the Cross family's coat of arms, for whom Eccle Riggs Manor was originally built in 1865. There are twelve beautifully furnished en-suite bedrooms all providing excellent facilities which include remote control colour TV with in-house video, and, for those who require, a baby listening service. The breakfast menu includes such delicacies as local smoked kippers or haddock which always prove popular. An excellent packed lunch is available on request or alternatively there is a wide selection of bar snacks served throughout the day. Finally, in the evening, you can relax in the bar, a large, comfortable room dominated by an impressive 16th century open fire place. Dinner at Eccle Riggs Manor is a feast, with an a la carte menu offering first class food accompanied by an extensive wine list featuring wines from all over the world. If you feel like pampering yourself during your stay, you can make an appointment with the qualified masseuse who visits the hotel daily, providing a full range of beauty treatments, whilst for those with more energy, there is a heated indoor swimming pool. Whatever your leisure pursuits, Eccle Riggs Manor is ideally situated with Lakes Coniston and Windermere within easy reach for sailing or water ski-ing. A quiet word with the receptionist can easily sort out a days fishing nearby, and a family outing on the steam railway is lovely way to tour the Lakes.

Eccle Riggs Manor Broughton-in-Furness   0229 716398

Greenodd, east of Broughton and north of Ulverston, is now a quiet village overlooking the Levens Estuary but it was once a major port with space for up to fifty ships. Stone, metal and ores produced in the Furness fells were transported from here to all over the world.

To the east is **Haverthwaite**, the start of the Haverthwaite and Lakeside Railway, which operates a steam train along the River Leven to Lake Windermere. In the Church of St Annes a mural tablet tells the tragic story of George Dickinson killed in Montevideo by a shot fired at another man. The bullet passed through the target's body but accidentally killed Dickinson.

The A590 Kendal to Barrow Roadpasses through Haverthwaite and here you will find **Oakbank**, a very pretty Lakeland house owned by Nancy Baker who provides first class, reasonably priced bed and breakfast accommodation. Set back from the road in its own wooded grounds the cottage has ample parking space and attractive gardens. The attractively furnished guest rooms all provide hot drinks facilities and colour TV, whilst the comfortable large conservatory gives a continental feel to breakfast time. Oakbank is ideally situated for touring the South Lakes, with Haverthwaite Steam Railway further down the road and many other popular tourist attractions within easy reach.

Oakbank   *Haverthwaite*   *05395 31009*

Leaving Haverthwaite in the direction of Kendal, turn right onto the B5278, a country road which follows the sandy coast through the villages of Holker and Cark, where the magnificent railway viaduct on the coast line crosses the Levens Estuary to the fishing village of Flookburgh. Nearby is **Holker Hall**, formerly home of the Dukes of Devonshire and now lived in by the Cavendish Family, set in a splendid country estate and deer-park. It is famous for one of the best private libraries in England with over 3,500 volumes. It also has exquisite interiors with fine woodcarvings and decorated ceilings. Here you will find and embroidered panel, said to have been worked by Mary, Queen of Scots, a Victorian and Edwardian Kitchen exhibition and an animal house.

Holker Hall

A short walk from Holker Hall, by footpath, is Cartmel, one of the prettiest villages in Furness. Cartmel is a delightful cluster of houses and cottages set around a square, from which lead winding streets and arches into charming back yards. The village is dominated by the famous Cartmel Priory, founded in 1188 by Augustine Canons. According to legend, it was originally intended to be sited on nearby Mount Barnard, but St Cuthbert appeared in a vision to the monastic architect and ordered him to build the Priory between two springs of water. Next morning the foundation stones were to be found trickling in opposite directions and this is where the Church stands today.

Like all such monastic institutions, the Priory was disbanded in 1537 and several of its members were executed for participating in the Pilgrimage of Grace. Today, only the 14th century gatehouse and the Church of St Mary and St Michael have survived. Indeed, after the dissolution, only the south aisle was used as a parish church, but in 1620

207

Gatehouse, Cartmel Priory

George Preston of Holker began to restore the entire building, re-roofing it and presenting the church with the richly-carved black oak screens and stall canopies.

Apart from its glorious east window, one of its most noticeable features is the unique tower set diagonally on the tower stage. Inside, in the south-west corner of the church, is a door known as Cromwell's Door. The holes in it are said to have been made by indignant parishioners firing at Cromwellian soldiers who had stabled their horses in the nave. Parliamentary troops were in the area in 1643 and, indeed, fragments of lead were found in the wood during restoration work in 1955. Cartmel also has a charming race course and any Tourist Information Centre will give details of the meetings held here.

Boarbank Farm   Allithwaite   05395 34091

Near to Cartmel, you would be hard put to find more unusual or visually attractive self catering accommodation than that at **Boarbank Farm** in **Allithwaite**. Located off the B5277 just past Allithwaite village, this selection of beautiful apartments and cottages are what dream holidays are made of. Your hosts Harry and Jean Whiteman are very welcoming and are happy to supply you with information on local places to visit and things to do. The buildings are grouped around an elegant courtyard which is reached by driving through the magnificent clock tower archway. Each apartment and cottage has been thoughtfully restored to retain the building's original character, whilst offering every modern comfort , thus ensuring a truly memorable holiday for all who stay here.

Allithwaite was founded by the Vikings, and originally called 'Lilifr's Thwaite', thwaite being the Westmorland word for 'a clearing'. In the 17th century it boasted a corn mill, and later a brewery, now converted into pretty cottages.

209

Within the old manor of Allithwaite is Humphrey Head where, in the 18th and 19th centuries, visitors flocked to sample the waters of the Holy Well. The Yorkshire and Cumberland miners thought the the waters would heal the illnesses caused by their work.

Still on the Cartmel Peninsula, further along the B5277, on the fringes of Grange-over-Sands is a lovely house called **The Chateau**, where Jean and Roy Robinson provide first class bed and breakfast accommodation. This charming house is ideally situated for exploring the south Lakes area and the Robinsons' prices are very reasonable. A friendly couple, Jean and Roy will happily help you to plan your outings and have numerous books and maps for you to use. The three guest rooms, one with en-suite bathroom and colour TV, are very spacious and comfortable with hot drinks facilities. The main bathroom is huge and luxurious, whilst downstairs there is a large guest lounge with its own terrace offering lovely sea views.

The Chateau   *Grange-over-Sands*   *0539 532249*

Once a small coastal village, **Grange-over-Sands** was transformed into a fashionable resort by the coming of the Furness Railway linking it with Lancaster. Villas and hotels were built to take advantage of the exceptionally mild climate. Though the sands are not safe for bathing, this is more than compensated by the extensive promenade gardens along the sea-front. Due to the mild climate these boast rock-plants, alpines and even subtropical species. Away from the hotels, shops and cafes there are some lovely walks, none nicer than the path behind the town which climbs through the magnificent limestone woodlands, rich in wild flowers. The path leads to Hampsfell Summit and the Hospice, a little stone tower from which there is an unforgettale view of Morecambe Bay and the craggy peaks of the Lake District. The Hospice was provided by a pastor of Cartmel in the last century for the 'shelter and entertainment of wanderers'. An external flight of stairs leads to a flat roof and the viewing-point. See if you can work out the riddle scrawled on one of the walls! Grange is also the starting point of the 'Cistercian Way', an exceptionally interesting, thirty-seven mile footpath route through Furness to Barrow, linking many sites of Cistercian interest.

Graythwaite Manor Hotel Grange-over-Sands 05395 32001

For a taste of luxury and real olde worlde charm, look no further than **Graythwaite Manor Hotel** on Fernhill Road. This magnificent hotel, set on the hillside in 8 acres of landscaped gardens and woodland, oozes comfort and tranquility throughout. Graythwaite Manor is currently run by the third generation of Blakemores, who have made this into a first class hotel. The lounges are elegantly furnished with beautiful antiques and the added touch of fresh flowers, whilst in the comfortable dining room you can enjoy mouthwatering six course dinners with a menu which changes daily and a fine accompanying wine list. With tastefully furnished en-suite accommodation in 22 guest rooms and a variety of leisure facilities within the hotel grounds, your luxury break is complete.

The road through Grange joins up with the A590, where it is worth taking a left turn to High Newton for more dramatic views acorss the Kent Estuary which is spanned by a fifty-arch railway viaduct. It was built by the engineer James Brunless in 1856-7, who used deep-sunk iron piles on broad circular discs to hold the structure firm amidst the treacherous Kent quicksands. The Estuary is a haven for wildlife with over 133 species of birds having been recorded in recent years.

In the pretty village of **Witherslack** near **High Newton** you will find an absolute gem called **The Old Vicarage**. This family run country house hotel has won many awards for both the beautifully furnished and excellently equipped accomodation and the mouthwatering cuisine. These include the rare honour of the AA Red Star and Egon Ronay's 1993

211

Cheese Board of the Year award. This is more than just a hotel, it is also a first class place to eat. In addition to gourmet menus and over 200 wines to choose from, The Old Vicarage has its own cheese menu and specialises in regional cheeses. The service and standard of this quiet hotel are what you might expect in one of the major commercial chains, but the pleasantly informal atmosphere makes The Old Vicarage a very rare find indeed.

The Old Vicarage   Witherslack   05395 52381

On the far bank of the Kent Estuary is the quiet town of **Arnside**, with its short but elegant promenade. Once a busy port with its own shipbuilding and sea-salt refining industries, the silting up of the estuary in the 19th century saw its decline. With Grange and nearby Silverdale (in Lancashire), it is now a favourite retirement destination and a quiet holiday resort.

Around Arnside itself there is a wonderful choice of country walks, particularly over and around Arnside Knott. This limestone headland, now a Nature Reserve rich in old woods and wild flowers, is part of the Arnside and Silverdale Area of Outstanding Natural Beauty. Knott comes from the Saxon word meaning 'rounded hill', which in this case rises 521ft above sea level and gives extensive views of the Lakeland fells, the Pennines and the coast. There is a beautiful path around the headland and along the shoreline past Blackstone Point. If you continue inland by quiet lanes or footpaths you soon reach Arnside Tower, another 14th-century pele tower. This particular one was built around 1375, during the reign of Edward III. It may have been part of the chain of towers designed to form a ring of protection for Morecambe Bay.

Beetham, on the A6 further inland, has an unusual 19th-century Post Office with a distinctive black-and-white studded door. Within earshot of a waterfall is the Church of St Michael and All Angels, approached through a pergola of rambling roses. The church dates from Saxon times and, during restoration work in 1834, a hoard of about a hundred old coins was discovered at the base of a pillar. The coins were from the reigns of Edward the Confessor, William the Conqueror and William Rufus. In the Civil War, the church was badly damaged, its windows smashed and effigies broken. However, a glass fragment of Henry IV in an ermine robe has survived.

Tucked away in the heart of the delightful village of Beetham is the charming **Wheatsheaf Hotel**. Overlooking Beetham's historic Norman church, the Hotel has been run by Margaret Shaw and her parents before her, for the past 30 years, and was originally built in 1609 as a coaching inn. It was ideally situated, lying only 100 yards off the A6, which was then the main road linking the South to Scotland, and it allowed travellers to rest and refresh themselves whilst the horses were changed. The Wheatsheaf is a popular and busy hotel, full of character, and although it has been obviously updated and refurbished, it has retained its original charm and exudes a warm, friendly atmosphere. The bar offers a wide choice of fine ales, and a varied selection of bar meals are available daily. On the first floor there is a cosy, intimate restaurant which provides an excellent, reasonably priced menu, including a variety of homemade pies and hotpots, tasty roasts, fresh fish and freshly made fruit tarts and meringue dishes, as well as an extensive cold buffet. Its popularity makes prior bookings advisable for weekend evenings or Sunday lunchtime. In addition to the fine fare on offer, Margaret also provides top class accommodation. There are six letting bedrooms, all en-suite, spacious and with that little extra personal touch, which makes The Wheatsheaf a lovely place to stay. Downstairs visitors should look out for the showcase which houses a vast selection of dolls that have been collected from all over the world.

The Wheatsheaf Hotel   Beetham   05395 62123

Heron Corn Mill, close by, is a restored and working water-mill, with fully operational grinding machinery. It is a good example of a traditional corn mill which operated for trade in a Westmorland farming area, and only ceased trading in 1955. The situation of Heron Mill is ideal, because a natural shelf of rock in the river Bela forms a waterfall, providing the necessaru head of water to drive the waterwheel. This made the site an obvious one when, in 1220, the Lords of the Manor of Haverback granted lands to the Canons of Coningshead for the erection of a corn mill. It is referred to several times in archives from the middle ages, and the land was transferred to Sir William Thorneburghe when Coningshead was destroyed at the Dissolution of the Monasteries in 1538.There is an exhibition about its history and the processes of milling.

The Ship Inn   Sandside   05395 63113

Heading north from Beetham along the A6, a turning to the left at Milnthorpe takes you onto the B5282, and after a mile or so, brings you to the **Ship Inn**, which stands on a sharp bend in the road at **Sandside**. The building dates from the 17th-century and takes its name from the ships which once transported iron ore across the bay from here. Formerly a coaching inn, it has been a pub for over 130 years and at one time brewed its own beer. Inside, there is a warm friendly atmosphere with oak-beamed ceilings and interesting 19th-century graffiti on the windows. Top quality food is served in the spacious lounge bar every lunchtime and evening, and there is also a pleasant games room and a large children's adventure playground to the rear.

Sandside sits on the banks of the Kent estuary, where in the Middle Ages, heavily-laden pack horses and drovers with sheep and cattle used to make hazardous crossings making their way up the coast into Cumbria, rather than taking the longer, but safer route via Levens. Hidden away in this little village is the charming **Kingfisher House and Restaurant**. It has been run by Tom and Milly Simister for the past nine years, and enjoys outstanding panoramic views, with beautiful evening sunsets over the Kent estuary, with its abundant birdlife including a colony of herons. Originally run just as a restaurant, Tom and Milly now provide top quality accommodation. There are four well furnished letting rooms, all en-suite with excellent facilities. The welcoming restaurant is truly first class with extensive menus to choose from, all offering mouthwatering dishes freshly prepared using local produce. This makes it very popular with locals and tourists alike, who know they are assured of excellent fare and value for money.

Kingfisher House   Sandside   05395 63909

Milnthorpe has been a market town since the 14th century. The River Bela runs by its side, past the comb mill - which makes combs from synthetic material these days, rather than horn or ivory as it used to - and through Dallam Tower park to meet up with the mouth of the River Kent.

'Eildon'   Milnthorpe   05395 63311

'Eildon' is a homely house on Church Street in Milnthorpe run by Rosemary Dale. It is spacious and well-decorated, with a peaceful, relaxing atmosphere. There is only one letting room available, so it is important to book in advance. At the front of the house is a large, well-tended garden, whilst to the rear ample car parking is provided. In addition to the usual facilities you would expect of a good bed and breakfast house, Rosemary offers wholefood/vegetarian specialities such as homemade wholemeal bread, whilst a muesli breakfast with fresh fruit is available for those who prefer it. Welcomed with homemade cake on your arrival, you will immediately be struck by the warm, home from home feel which makes 'Eildon' a lovely place to stay.

Veronica's Café and Sarah's Beestro on Park Road is a business run by mother and daughter, where the emphasis is on service with a smile. With its homely atmosphere, the cafe is a haven for cyclists, walkers and tourists in need of something to fill that gap. There are various filling breakfasts, toasted sandwiches, salads and other traditional cafe fare all made to order. Open every day, except Monday, from 9.00am to 5.30pm as a café, it becomes Sarah's Beestro, correctly spelt in this case, on Thursday, Friday and Saturday nights, from 7.00pm to 9.00pm. Bookings for the Beestro are preferred and you are advised to bring your own wine as the premises are unlicensed.

Veronica's Café   Milnthorpe   05395 63143

The Market Cross on the square is not actually a cross, but a column with ball finial set on limestone steps, which used to serve as a whipping post for wrongdoers. At the other end of the Square is the fountain, which was once the village well, and the spring can still be seen under the grating.

Standing in the heart of Milnthorpe at its centre crossroads is The **Bull's Head Hotel**, one of only three inns left in this once busy village that used to boast seven. Run by Janis and Mick, the Hotel has been completely upgraded and redecorated to provide cosy, friendly bars, a comfortable lounge room and three spacious, well-decorated letting rooms, all with tea and coffee making facilities. The Bull's head is open from 12 noon to 11pm daily except Sundays, and in the bar guests can enjoy a wide range of excellent ales and good home-cooked food.

The Bull's Head Hotel   Milnthorpe   05395 62133

For the more active among you, we recommend **Trekkers Riding Centre** at **Hale**, near Milnthorpe, which is run by Mandy Kennedy and has horses to suit every age and ability, offering rides from one hour to a full day's duration. In addition to the usual treks around the lovely country lanes, Mandy offers pub rides, barbeque rides and even weekend adventure rides. Just 200 yards away from the Centre is **Hall-More Trout Fishery**, run by Jeff Brookes. For those who prefer the more sedate pastime of fishing, this is the perfect location. There is a 31/2 acre lake, well stocked with rainbow and brown trout. If you have the skill, you can take home your catch, depending on how long you fish for, but whatever your ability, Hall-More provides good sport in beautiful surroundings.

Trekkers Riding Centre   Hale   05395 63265

217

Those looking for a convenient camping or caravan base, or bed and breakfast, Carnforth, just across the border into Lancashire, is well-situated.

Capernwray House at Carnforth is a non-smoking establishment run by Melanie and Roy Smith, set in five and a half acres of beautiful countryside on the borders of Cumbria and Lancashire. A very attractive house, it has three beautifully decorated letting bedrooms, all en-suite and well equipped. There is a large, comfortable lounge to relax in and an airy dining room where breakfast is served. Outside to the rear of the house is a small, select caravan park where the facilities include a modern toilet block with showers, basins, shaver points and laundry room. There is also a chemical toilet disposal point, a telephone, and electric hook up points throughout the park as well as a lovely children's play area.

Carnforth is easily accessible, and particularly convenient for visitors to this region from the south.

Capernwray Country House   Carnforth   0524 732363

The South Cumbrian Coast

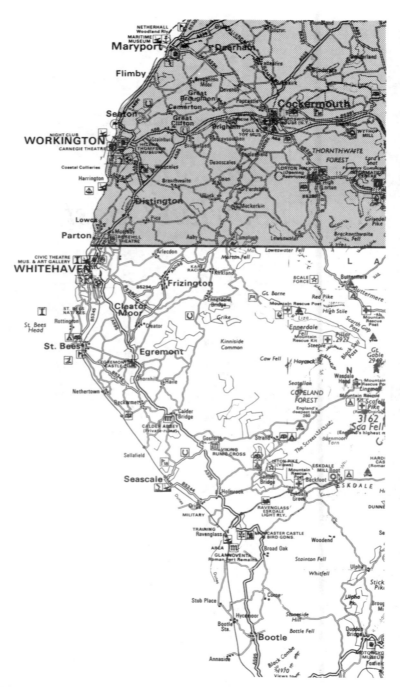

Index

Boot

The South Cumbrian Coast

Calder Abbey

CHAPTER EIGHT

The South Cumbrian Coast

The section of Cumbria's coast and hinterland stretching down from St Bees Head to the Duddon Estuary has its own identity and quiet charm. It is a coast dominated by small, 19th century, iron-mining communities set against the romantic outline of the Lakeland Fells and the grey-blue waters of the Irish Sea. This area is most brilliantly captured in the verse and prose of Millom poet, Norman Nicholson.

Millom stands at the mouth of the River Duddon on the banks of the estuary, with the 1970ft Black Combe Fell behind it. Like neighbouring towns in this region, it grew with the development of the iron industry, and the town's Folk Museum tells its history. The Museum also contains a permanent memorial to Norman Nicholson which tells of his books of verse and prose on local life and customs.

From Millom, the A5093 leads to Broughton-in-Furness, further along the estuary.

The Dower House High Duddon   *0229 716279*

The Dower House at Duddon Bridge, just before you reach Broughton, is a beautiful late Victorian mansion which has been sympathetically converted to combine guest house facilities with self catering accommo-

225

dation. This elegant establishment stands in six acres of secluded woodland and gardens, with abundant wildlife and tumbling streams, which also provide the water supply. The apartments are reached via the entrance hall to the main house, which features a magnificent fireplace with a carved wood surround, and off the hall there is a comfortable residents' lounge and bar. Each apartment is excellently equipped and completely self-contained, but evening meals are available if required. Children are very well catered for, with a comprehensive Games Room, as well as the delightful grounds to explore.

The area of coastline between Kirksanton and the ancient Roman port of Ravenglass is the only part of the National Park to come in contact with the sea. Approximately midway along this stretch, turning coastwards off the A595 at Bootle, after a mile you will come to the **Station Hotel**, a first-rate inn and eating place which stands adjacent to the Barrow-Carlisle line at **Bootle Station**. Originally built by the railway company in the late 19th-century, the hotel lies a mile from the beach and within one-and-a-half hour's drive of all the major lakes. Proprietors Rita and Tom Edmondson have four comfortable en suite bedrooms available and serve a wide range of delicious meals both at lunchtimes and in the evenings.

Station Hotel   Bootle   0229 718207

Continuing on the A595, you will reach Ravenglass, which lies on the estuary of three rivers - the Esk, the Mite and the Irt. Because of its sheltered position, Ravenglass became an important naval-base for the Romans in the 2nd century. It was a supply point for the military zone around Hadrian's Wall. Except for a remarkable Bath House, little remains now of their large fort of 'Glannaventra' on the cliffs above the village. **The Bath House** is an impressive building and one of the best surviving Roman structures in England, with walls over 12ft high.

In the 18th century Ravenglass was a base for smugglers bringing contraband in from coastal ships - tobacco and French brandy. Today the estuary has silted up but there are still scores of small boats and the village is a charming resort, full of atmosphere. The layout has changed little since the 16th century. The main street is paved with sea-pebbles and leads up from a shingle beach. Once, iron-ore was brought to the estuary by narrow-gauge railway from the mines near Boot, in Eskdale, about eight miles away.

Chemist sign

The Ravenglass and Eskdale Railway, which runs for seven miles up the lovely Mite and Esk River valleys, was first opened to passengers in 1876 since when it has survived several threats of extinction. In 1915 it was converted from 3ft-gauge track to a new miniature 15in-gauge and carried passengers and freight - which later included granite - between Ravenglass and Dalegarth. However, towards the end of the 1950s, the closure of the granite quarries seemed to spell disaster for 'T'laal Ratty' (as the railway is affectionately known). At the auction of the railway in 1960 a band of enthusiasts outbid the scrap-dealers and a company was formed to keep the little railway running.

Today there are twelve locomotives, both steam and diesel, and 300,000 people a year come from all over the world to ride on 'T'laal Ratty' and enjoy the splendour of Eskdale. It is still the best way to explore Mitedale and Eskdale, enchanting both young and old.

At Ravenglass there is a fascinating small museum of iron-mining and the history of the line. The station has a souvenir shop and refreshment room. The 100-year old British Railways station building was converted into the Ratty Arms, the railway's own pub.

Muncaster Mill, a mile or so up the River Mite, is reached by Eskdale trains and has working machinery dating from the late 18th century. A mill has stood here since the 15th century, though the present building only dates from around 1700. It was carefully restored by the Railway Company in 1976-8 and is powered by a great, overshot water-wheel. It still produces a wide variety of stone-ground, wholemeal flours.

Muncaster Castle   Ravenglass   0229 717614

A mile or so east of **Ravenglass** stands **Muncaster Castle**, an impressive castellated mansion which has been owned by the Pennington family since 1208. It has grown from the original Pele Tower built on Roman foundations to the impressive structure that can be seen today. Outstanding features are the Great Hall, Salvin's octagonal library and the drawing room with its barrel ceiling. Muncaster contains many treasures including beautiful furniture, tapestries, silver and porcelain. In 1464, King Henry VI sheltered here from his enemies after losing the Battle of Hexham. In gratitude, he left his glass enamelled drinking bowl, now known as the *Luck of Muncaster*, saying that the Pennington family will live at the Castle as long as the bowl remains unbroken. The woodland gardens cover 77 acres and command spectacular views of the Lakeland Fells. From mid-March to June, the famous rhododendrons, azaleas and camellias are at their best. The grounds also contain a fascinating owl centre. Here, visitors can meet the birds daily at 2.30pm (April to end October) when a talk is given on the work of the centre, and weather permitting, the owls display their flying skills. The gardens and owl centre are open daily throughout the year; castle open afternoons end-March to end-October (closed Mondays).

The **Muncaster Country Guest House** is situated adjacent to the Muncaster Castle estate. Owners Roger and Mu Putnam have converted the former local primary school into an extremely friendly and comfortable haven for walkers, climbers, anglers and those touring the beautiful countryside of Eskdale, Wasdale and the Cumbrian coast by car. The

Stanley Ghyll

guesthouse is set within a large attractive garden and has two pleasant sitting rooms with open fires, eight letting bedrooms (some with en suite bathrooms) and a comfortable self-catering apartment. Roger is the former leader of the local mountain rescue team and leads walks in the surrounding countryside and the central fells for visitors wishing to explore the area on foot.

Muncaster Country Guest House   Ravenglass   0229 717693

At Holmrook, just north of Ravenglass, turn west off the main road and follow the B5344 towards the coast. Having passed through the pleasant village of Drigg, follow the signs to **Drigg Station**, the home of Kathleen Egglestone's craft shop, **Spindle Craft**. The waiting room and ticket office of this handsome Victorian building now house a fascinating collection of crafts, some handmade, and works of art including pottery, designer knitwear, haematite jewellery, Liberty gifts and original paintings. The shop is also an agent for Ashford spinning wheels and retails woollen garments knitted in the village. Open daily 9.30am-5.30pm, all year round. Closed Thursdays between Christmas and Easter.

Spindle Craft   Drigg   09467 24335

The Woolpack, a fine, family-run inn recommended by Egon Ronay, stands in the tranquility of the picturesque Eskdale Valley. The building, once a working farm, dates back to the 17th century and has spacious rooms traditionally decorated. Antique furniture, oak panels, and large, old fireplaces all combine to create a warm and relaxing atmosphere of great charm. Anne and Fred Fox are renowned for their Cumbrian hospitality and guests staying at The Woolpack will find cosy well-equipped rooms and a residents' lounge-bar with an open fire. The Dalesman Bar, popular with both passing fellwalkers and local people who come in for a chat, is known for its extensive range of draught beers, including Real Ale, home-cooked snacks and a selection of traditional pub games. The Woolpack Country Kitchen restaurant with its splendid open range, provides a substantial and excellent menu of traditional food. The fresh locally bought produce, all home-cooked, is often supplemented by the Inn's own vegetable garden.

The Woolpack Inn   Holmbrook   09467 23230

For that perfect break away from it all, whatever your leisure interests, **Stanley Ghyll House** in Eskdale is ideal. One of thirteen properties in the British Isles owned by Countrywide Holidays Association, who 100 years ago pioneered walking and special interest holidays, this simply furnished Victorian house provides a very comfortable base from which to scale nearby peaks such as the Scafells, or to follow the area's vast network of footpaths. The Roman fort at Hardknott and the fort and bath house beyond Muncaster are both easily accessible from here, and an added attraction is The Ratty Steam Railway, which makes regular stops just outside the house. Guests spending a week or more here receive a free runabout ticket to use on the railway during their stay. Whilst accommodation can be booked direct with the house, for special interest and walking holidays telephone 061 225 1000.

231

The village of **Boot** lies at the eastern end of the Ravenglass and Eskdale Railway and is a wonderful place to visit whether arriving by train or car. It is a gentle walk from the station at Eskdale, and is a delightful village, with its pub, post office, museum watermill and nearby St Catherine's Church in its riverside setting.

Stanley Ghyll House   Boot   09467 23327

One particular place of interest here is the **Fold End Gallery**, a converted sheep barn which houses an impressive collection of work by some of the best artists and craftspeople currently working in Cumbria. As well as a carefully selected range of original oils, watercolours and etchings, the gallery contains a constantly changing display of individual welded steel sculptures, bronzes and turned wood pieces. There is also a range of attractive stoneware and earthenware pottery and a fine collection of silver, enamel and haematite jewellery. Open Tuesdays to Sundays, 10am to 5.30pm.

Fold End Gallery   Boot   09467 23213

Further north along the A595 is **Gosforth**, famous for its 15ft-high

Viking cross which towers above the huddled gravestones in a peaceful churchyard. Carved from red sandstone and clearly influenced by both Christian and pagan tradition, it depicts the crucifixion, the deeds of Norse gods and 'Yggdrasil', the World Ash Tree that Norsemen believed supported the universe. St Mary's is built on the site of an earlier Norman church and contains several other ancient relics. The Chinese Bell on the western window-sill of the church was captured in 1841 at Anunkry, a fort on the River Canton. Look out, too, for the delightful carved faces on the chancel arch and a cork tree planted in 1833.

Walkmill Garden Centre Gosforth   09467 25293

At any time of year, a visit to Gosforth's **Walkmill Gardens** is well worthwhile. Keen gardeners can browse over the extensive range of plants, many of them from John W Matterson's own nursery of twenty years standing. All tastes are catered for in the large retail area of the garden centre which stocks a huge range of top quality garden products. There is also an interesting selection of specialist goods including dried and silk flowers, flower-arranging accessories and attractive gifts for all ages. Particular favourites amongst the excellent range of local Cumbrian products are the farmhouse biscuits, preserves and home-produced honey from John's own hives.

Visitors to Gosforth will discover a taste of the Orient when they visit **Gosforth Hall Hotel**. Situated next to St. Mary's church, the hotel was originally built in 1673 as a home for a prominent local couple, Robert and Isabel Copley. Today the proprietors John and Suda Westoby have developed Westo's Thai restaurant on the ground floor, where you can sample authentic Thai cooking prepared by Suda, herself a native Thailander and excellent cook. Within the hotel, which took 15 years to build, the accommodation is very comfortable and there is the additional attraction of an outdoor swimming pool and Sky TV. Guests who dine at Westo's get the added bonus of overnight bed and breakfast for only £10.75 per person on Fridays, Saturdays and Sundays.

Gosforth Hall Hotel   Gosforth   09467 25322

Nether Wasdale is a tiny, tranquil Cumbrian village nestling at the foot of Wasdale, just east of Gosforth. Here you will find Low Wood Hall, a fine example of Lakeland Victorian architecture, which stands in well tended gardens on the lower slopes of the fells. Graham and 'Xandra Brassington are friendly hosts who have succeeded in creating a relaxed and welcoming atmosphere. The Hall has been sympathetically modernised to provide 20th century comforts such as central heating, whilst still retaining its Victorian character with original gas chandeliers, beautiful marble fireplaces and a wealth of stained glass. The guest rooms all provide en-suite facilities, and downstairs guests can make use of the comfortable lounge bar, spacious billiard room, drawing room, and lovely dining room which overlooks the gardens and fells.

Low Wood Hall   Nether Wasdale   09467 26287

Egremont is dominated by its Norman Castle standing high above the town, overlooking the lovely River Ehen to the south and the market place to the north. The castle was built between 1130 and 1140 by William de Meschines on the site of a former Danish fortification. The most complete part still standing is a Norman arch that once guarded the drawbridge entrance. Nearby is an unusual four-sided sundial and the stump of the old market-cross dating from the early 13th century.

Wordsworth's poem, 'The Horn of Egremont Castle', is based on a local legend from the Middle Ages. It is said that a great horn hanging in the castle could only be blown by the rightful lord. In the 13th century Hubert de Lucy arranged to have the rightful lord, his brother Eustace, murdered so that he could claim his title. The plot misfired and during the celebration feast to mark Hubert's inheritance, Eustace returned to blow the horn. Hubert, wisely, fled to a monastery.

Wastwater

Egremont's prosperity was based on the good quality of its local iron-ore. Today it still retains a strong 19th century air with its simple, colour-washed houses opening directly onto the street. Wander down the wide, tree-lined main street towards the Parish Church of St Mary and St Michael, a superb example of Victorian Gothic architecture.

In September every year the town celebrates its Crab Fair. The fair dates from the 13th century when crab-apples were distributed to by-standers. Now Worcestershire apples are thrown from a lorry which drives down the main street. The fair is usually celebrated with traditional sports which include wrestling and hound-trailing. The highlight is the World Gurning Championship, in which each 'gurner' puts his head through a horse collar and pulls an ugly face - the ugliest being declared the winner!

There are some particularly fine walks from Egremont, over the fells, passing through small villages like Wilton and Haile. Haile stands on a hill overlooking a simple, modern church which has ancient stones incorporated into the fabric, some with Roman inscriptions. A fine avenue of beech trees leads to a stone gate-house and archway through which can be seen 16th century **Haile Hall**.

Near the small, grey, 19th century settlement of Calder Bridge is **Calder Abbey**, linked to the village by an attractive footpath. It was founded by monks of Savigny in 1134 but amalgamated with the Cistercians of Furness Abbey when it was ransacked by the Scots a few years later. After the Dissolution the monastery buildings lapsed slowly into the present-day romantic ruin. Part of the tower and west doorway remain, with some of the chancel and transept, but sadly these are unsafe and have to be viewed from the road. The River Calder rises on Caw Fell south of Ennerdale Water. Monks Bridge, the oldest packhorse bridge in Cumbria, was built for the monks and has no parapets in order to accommodate the panniers, or sacks, of the loaded pack-horses.

St Bees Head, a red sandstone bluff, forms one of the most dramatic natural features along the entire coast of North-west England. It is four miles of towering, precipitous cliffs of 'St Bee's Sandstone', the red rock which is so characteristic of Cumbria. Far out to sea, on the horizon, can be seen the grey shadow of the Isle of Man, and on a clear day, the shimmering outline of the Irish coast. From St Bees Head the 190 mile Coast to Coast Walk starts on its long journey across the Pennines to Robin Hood's Bay on the East Coast.

Appleby Castle and Rare Breeds Centre

Long before the first lighthouse was built in 1822, there was a beacon on the headland to warn and guide passing ships away from the rocks. The present lighthouse dates from 1866-7, built after an earlier one was destroyed by fire. St Bees Head is now an important Nature Reserve and the cliffs are crowded with guillemots, razorbills, kittiwakes, gulls, gannets and skuas and you'll find Observation and Information Points all along the headland. There is a superb walk of about eight miles along the coastal footpath around the headland from St Bees to Whitehaven.

St. Bees

A short walk from the headland is the small village of St Bees which lies huddled in a deep, slanting bowl in the cliffs, fringed by a shingle beach. The village is a delightful place to explore, with its main street winding up the hillside between old farms and cottages. It derives its name from 'St Bega', daughter of an Irish king who, on the day she was meant to marry a Norse prince, was miraculouly transpsorted by an angel to the Cumbrian coast. According to legend, on Midsummer Night's Eve, St Bega asked the pagan Lord Egremont for some land on which to found a Nunnery. Cunningly, he promised her only as much land as was covered by snow the following morning. But on Midsummer's Day, three square miles of land were blanketed white with snow and here she founded her Priory.

Soon after, however, forced to flee from her rejected suitor, she took

237

refuge in the the King of Northumbria's court; there she helped to found Whitby Abbey. The Priory at St Bees grew in size and importance until it was destroyed by the Danes in the 10th century. The Benedictines later re-established the Priory in 1129. The Priory Church of St Mary and St Bega is all that is now left but, although it has been substantially altered, there is still a magnificent Norman arch. Look out for the pre-Conquest, carved Beowulf Stone on a lintel between the Church and the Vicarage, showing St Michael killing a dragon. Close by the Church are the charming Abbey cottages and St Bees school with its handsome clock-tower. The school was founded in 1583 by Edmund Grindal, Archbishop of Canterbury under Elizabeth I, and the son of a local farmer. The original red sandstone quadrangle bears his coat-of-arms and the bridge he gave to the village is still in use.

The Queen's Hotel   St. Bees   0946 822287

The Queen's Hotel is a handsome 17th-century free house and hotel which stands in St. Bees' ancient main street. Inside, there is a wonderful traditional atmosphere with oak-beamed ceilings and the conspicuous absence of a juke box or fruit machines. The bars offer three cask-conditioned ales and a range of over seventy malt whiskies (those managing to sample fifty during their stay become members of the '50 Malt Club'). Delicious, freshly-prepared meals are served in the panelled dining area adjacent to the bar. Recently refurbished, the Queen's offers fifteen guest bedrooms, all with en-suite facilities, colour televisions and beverage making facilities. There is also an attractive secluded beer garden at the rear.

Inland from St Bee's, **Ennerdale** is truly a hidden place. It is tranquil and quiet offering lake shores, river banks, valley paths and forest tracks which together offer a tremendous variety of walks suitable for all ages and capabilities. Other activities available include fishing, canoeing, bird watching and pony trekking. Wainwright's coast to coast walk runs the whole length of Ennerdale and the general consensus is that this section is by far the most beautiful.

The Shepherd's Arms Hotel   Ennerdale   0946 861249

In the centre of this lovely village you will find an ideal base from which to explore this unspoilt area at The **Shepherd's Arms Hotel**. There are six comfortable guest rooms available, some en-suite and two with four-poster bed. The licensed restaurant provides good home-cooked food, using fresh local produce, whilst the cosy bar serves real ale from the local brewery and offers an extensive wine list.

Routen Llama Farm   Ennerdale   0946 861270

The Routen Llama Farm stands in an idyllic position in the heart of spectacular Ennerdale. Originally a Viking farm, the present farmhouse was constructed in the 1850s near the lakeside. As well as being a working llama and rare breeds farm with a herd of over twenty llamas, miniature Dexter cattle, Vietnamese pot-bellied pigs and Polwarth sheep, this delightful establishment also operates as a superb guesthouse. Two of its four bedrooms have en suite facilities and all have colour televisions and tremendous views of Ennerdale Water. Delicious four-course

239

Gosforth Cross

dinners are served each evening in a relaxed dinner party atmosphere. Accommodation is unsuitable for smokers and young children. Owners Tricia and Michael Wakem let the original farmhouse as a charming three-bedroomed holiday cottage sleeping six.

Whitehaven was established in the 12th century as a harbour for use by the monks of nearby St Bees Priory, but most of the town was developed by the Lowther family to carry coal from their mines near the coast. In the mid-18th century Whitehaven was an important port, its trade based on coal and other cargo business. It was a larger port than Liverpool at that time and ranked only third in national importance after London and Bristol. It imported tobacco from Virginia, exported coal to Ireland and saw the emigration of settlers to the New World. However, in the days of large iron-steamships, its shallow draught halted expansion and the port declined in favour of Liverpool and Southampton. For that reason much of the attractive harbour area - now full of pleasure craft and fishing smacks - and older parts of the town remain unchanged.

There used to be two parish churches in Whitehaven - St James and St Nicholas. St James stands on a hill at the top of Queen Street, was built between 1752-3 and contains one of the finest Georgian church interiors in Cumbria. St Nicholas Church, on Lowther Street, was largely destroyed by fire in 1971 but an attractive garden now surrounds the ruins. A plaque marks the burial place of Mildred Warner Gale, better known as George Washington's grandmother, who died in 1700 and is buried here.

The Beilby 'Slavery' Goblet

There is a fascinating Town 'Walkabout' Trail and a Nature Trail around Tom Hurd Rock, above the town. Leaflets can be obtained from the Information Centre in St Nicholas Tower in Lowther Street. There is also the particularly interesting Whitehaven Museum and Art Gallery.

The Museum deals with the history of the whole of Copeland (the District of Cumbria in which Whitehaven lies) with special emphasis on its mining and maritime history. The displays reflect the many aspects of this harbour-borough with a collection which includes paintings, locally made pottery, ship models and navigational instruments, miners lamps and surveying equipment. The Beilby '*Slavery*' Goblet, part of the museum's collection, is one of the masterpieces of English glass-making and is probably the finest example of its kind in existence.

If you take a stroll down the West Strand in Whitehaven you will come across an attractive pub, **The Royal Standard**, a listed building which used to be the Royal Theatre. The building has to carry the royal coat of arms and if royalty should ever pay a visit here, the hosts would have to give up their beds for them! This recently decorated "regal" establishment serves Jennings bitter, excellent real ale from the local brewery, and is a particularly popular watering hole with the local fishermen. As well as fine ale, visitors here can also enjoy hearty breakfasts and homecooked bar meals at lunchtime and in the evening.

The Royal Standard   *Whitehaven*   *0946 691130*

The town is interesting in other ways. It still has a 'grid iron' pattern of streets dating back to the 17th century, a layout that can claim to be the first planned town in Britain. Many of the fine Georgian buildings in the centre have been restored and Lowther Street is a particularly impressive thoroughfare. Also of note is the harbour pier built by canal engineer, John Rennie, and considered to be one of the finest in Britain.

The North Cumbrian Coast

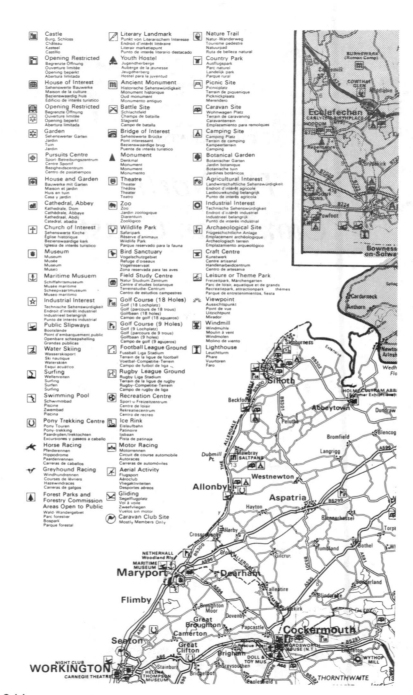

Castle — Burg, Schloss / Château / Kasteel / Castillo

Opening Restricted — Begrenzte Öffnung / Ouverture limitée / Opening beperkt / Abertura limitada

House of Interest — Sehenswerte Bauwerke / Maison de la culture / Bezienswaardig huis / Edificio de interés turístico

Opening Restricted — Begrenzte Öffnung / Ouverture limitée / Opening beperkt / Abertura limitada

Garden — Sehenswerter Garten / Jardin / Tuin / Jardín

Pursuits Centre — Sport-Betreibungszentrum / Centre Sportif / Bezighedscentrum / Centro de pasatiempos

House and Garden — Bauwerke mit Garten / Maison et jardin / Huis en tuin / Casa y jardín

Cathedral, Abbey — Kathedrale, Dom / Cathédrale, Abbaye / Kathedraal, Abdij / Catedral, abadía

Church of Interest — Sehenswerte Kirche / Eglise historique / Bezienswaardige kerk / Iglesia de interés turístico

Museum — Museum / Musée / Museum / Museo

Maritime Museum — Schiffahrtsmuseum / Musée maritime / Scheepvaartmuseum / Museo marítimo

Industrial Interest — Technische Sehenswürdigkeit / Endroit d'intérêt industriel / Industrieel belangrijk / Punto de interés industrial

Public Slipways — Bootslände / Point d'embarquement public / Openbare scheepshelling / Grandes públicas

Water Skiing — Wasserskisport / Ski nautique / Waterskiën / Esqui acuático

Surfing — Wellenreiten / Surfing / Surfen / Surfing

Swimming Pool — Schwimmbad / Piscine / Zwembad / Piscina

Pony Trekking Centre — Pony Touren / Pony-trekking / Paardrijden/trektochten / Excursiones y paseos a caballo

Horse Racing — Pferderennen / Hippodrome / Paardenrennen / Carreras de caballos

Greyhound Racing — Windhundrennen / Courses de lévriers / Hazewindrennen / Carreras de galgos

Forest Parks and Forestry Commission Areas Open to Public — Wald-Wandergebiet / Parc forestier / Bospark / Parque forestal

Literary Landmark — Punkt von Literarischem Interesse / Endroit d'intérêt littéraire / Literair marketlepunt / Punto de interés literario destacado

Youth Hostel — Jugendherberge / Auberge de la jeunesse / Jeugdherberg / Hostel para la juventud

Ancient Monument — Historische Sehenswürdigkeit / Monument historique / Oud monument / Monumento antiguo

Battle Site — Schlachtfeld / Champs de bataille / Slagveld / Campo de batalla

Bridge of Interest — Sehenswerte Brücke / Pont historique / Bezienswaardige brug / Puente de interés turístico

Monument — Denkmal / Monument / Monument / Monumento

Theatre — Theater / Théâtre / Theater / Teatro

Zoo — Zoo / Jardin zoologique / Dierentuin / Zoológico

Wildlife Park — Safaripark / Réserve d'animaux / Wildlife Park / Parque reservado para la fauna

Bird Sanctuary — Vogelschutzgebiet / Refuge d'oiseaux / Vogelreservaat / Zona reservada para las aves

Field Study Centre — Natur Studium Zentrum / Centre d'études botanique / Terreinstudie-Centrum / Centro de estudios campestres

Golf Course (18 Holes) — Golf (18 Lochplatz) / Golf (parcours de 18 trous) / Golfbaan (18 holes) / Campo de golf (18 agujeros)

Golf Course (9 Holes) — Golf (9 Lochplatz) / Golf (parcours de 9 trous) / Golfbaan (9 holes) / Campo de golf (9 agujeros)

Football League Ground — Fussball Liga Stadium / Terrain de la ligue de football / Voetbal-Competitie-Terrein / Campo de futbol de liga

Rugby League Ground — Rugby Liga Stadium / Terrain de la ligue de rugby / Rugby-Competitie-Terrein / Campo de rugby de liga

Recreation Centre — Sport-u Freizeitzentrum / Centre de loisir / Rekreatiecentrum / Centro de recreo

Ice Rink — Eislaufbahn / Patinoire / Ijsbaan / Pista de patinaje

Motor Racing — Motorrennen / Circuit de course automobile / Autoraces / Carreras de automóviles

Aerial Activity — Flugsport / Aéroclub / Vliegaktiviteiten / Deportes aéreos

Gliding — Segelflugplatz / Vol à voile / Zweefvliegen / Vuelos sin motor

Caravan Club Site — Mostly Members Only

Nature Trail — Natur-Wanderweg / Tourisme pedestre / Natuurpad / Ruta de belleza natural

Country Park — Ausflugspark / Parc naturel / Landelijk park / Parque rural

Picnic Site — Picnicplatz / Terrain de piquenique / Picknickplaats / Merendero

Caravan Site — Wohnwagen Platz / Terrain de caravaning / Caravanterrein / Emplazamiento para remolques

Camping Site — Camping Platz / Terrain de camping / Kampeerterrein / Camping

Botanical Garden — Botanischer Garten / Jardin botanique / Botanische tuin / Jardines botánicos

Agricultural Interest — Landwirtschaftliche Sehenswürdigkeit / Endroit d'intérêt agricole / Landbouwkundig belangrijk / Punto de interés agrícola

Industrial Interest — Technische Sehenswürdigkeit / Endroit d'intérêt industriel / Industrieel belangrijk / Punto de interés industrial

Archaeological Site — Frügeschichtliche Anlage / Emplacement archéologique / Archeologisch terrein / Emplazamiento arqueológico

Craft Centre — Kunstwerk / Centre artisanal / Handenarbeidcentrum / Centro de artesanía

Leisure or Theme Park — Freizeitpark, Märchengarten / Parc de loisir, aquatique et de grands thèmes / Recreatiepark, attractionpark / Parque de entretenimientos, fiesta

Viewpoint — Aussichtspunkt / Point de vue / Uitzichtspunt / Mirador

Windmill — Windmühle / Moulin à vent / Windmolen / Molino de viento

Lighthouse — Leuchtturm / Phare / Vuurtoren / Faro

Index

Whitehaven

The North Cumbrian Coast

Silloth

CHAPTER NINE

The North Cumbrian Coast

Workington, the largest town on the Cumbrian coast, stands at the mouth of the River derwent on the site of a former Roman fort of 'Gabrosentum'. Its prosperity was founded on three great Cumbrian industries - coal, iron and shipping. As early as 1650 coal was being mined here and, by the end of the 18th century, Workington was a major port exporting coal as well as smelting iron-ore. Many of the underground coal seams extended far out to sea. In later years Workington was famous for its fine-quality steel, and it is still the place in Britain where most railway lines are manufactured. It also has a national reputation for the buses and lorries that are built just outside the town.

Workington Hall   Workington   0900 604351

Workington Hall was the Curwen family seat for over 600 years and has a fascinating history. Originally built up around a 14th century Peel Tower, the Hall was developed over the years with extensive alterations being made in the eighteenth century by the then lord of the manor, John Christian Curwen. Now a stabilised ruin, there are commemorative plaques which give a taste of the Hall's history. The most famous visitor to the Hall was Mary Queen of Scots who sought refuge here when she

249

fled from Scotland in 1558. She stayed for a few days during which time she wrote a letter to her cousin Queen Elizabeth I seeking advice and assistance. The letter is now housed in the British Museum.

Helena Thompson Museum   Workington   0900 604351

The Helena Thompson Museum situated on Park End Road is fascinating place to visit with its displays telling the story of Workington's coal mining, shipbuilding, iron and steel industries for which the town became internationally renowned. The Georgian Room gives an insight into the variety of decorative styles which were popular between 1714 and 1830, with displays of beautiful cut-glass tableware, porcelain from China, and period pieces of furniture. Bequeathed to the town by Miss Helena Thompson, M.B.E., J.P., the museum was opened in 1949 and contains some of her own family heirlooms. One particularly interesting museum exhibit is the Clifton Dish, a locally produced 18th century piece of slipware pottery and displays show the links between this local industry and the famous Staffordshire pottery families.

The Royal Yew   Dean   0946 861342

Dean, some six miles east of Workington, is a charming village full of old houses and farms. The churchyard is entered through a lychgate and outside the church is an ancient preaching-cross probably dating from the 12th century. Three original 15th-century gargoyles, one face downwards, decorate the south wall.

Dean is signposted off the A5086 Cockermouth to Egremont road, and is the picturesque location of **The Royal Yew**, a charming country pub run by Alastair Chalmers. Open seven days a week, this cosy, welcoming establishment is renowned locally for its superb bar food and justly so. The menu is varied and imaginative, with best selling dishes such as Old Peculiar Pie, a home made steak and mushroom pie, and Pavlova the most popular dessert. There are a wide range of steak dishes, as well as other main courses, and a children's menu. All are very reasonably priced, and with the accompanying extensive wine list, which includes wines from all over the world, The Royal Yew makes the perfect venue for lunch or dinner.

Maryport, along the coast north of Workington, is a town rich in interest. The old part is full of narrow streets, neo-classical, Georgian architecture and quaint, picturesque neeks which contrast with sudden, surprising views of the sea.

Originally it was a small village known as Ellenfoot. The Romans built their fort of 'Alauna' on a clifftop just north of the present town, as part of their chain of defences against the Picts and traces of it still remain. Later excavations revealed a number of Roman altars that had been buried in shallow pits near the fort.

Maryport Maritime Museum   Maryport   0900 604351

Modern Maryport dates from the 18th century when Humphrey Senhouse, a local landowner, developed the harbour to export coal from his mines, naming the new port after his wife, Mary. Over the next century it became a busy port as well as a ship-building centre, boats having to be launched broadside because of the narrowness of the harbour channel. The town declined, along with the mining industry, from the 1930's onwards. However, it is now enjoying a well-earned revival, with newly-restored Georgian quaysides, steep cobbled streets, clifftop paths, sandy beaches and a harbour full of fishing boats and colourful pleasure craft.

Maryport lies on the Solway Firth just 27 miles from Carlisle. The town's extensive maritime history is preserved in the vast array of obects, pictures and models on display at **Maryport Maritime Museum**. Here you can follow the stories of mutineer Fletcher Christian of 'Bounty' fame, or seafarer Thomas Ismay who established the White Star Line which built the ill-fated Titanic. You can learn about a fascinating local man Joseph Peile, who sailed on the 'Cinq Ports' with Alexander Selkirk. It was during this voyage that Selkirk, on whom Daniel Defoe modelled 'Robinson Crusoe', was marooned on the island of Juan Fernandez. All this and much more besides, makes Maryport Maritime Museum a fascinating place to visit.

Maryport Steamships   Maryport   0900 604351

Just down the road from the Maritime Museum, at Elizabeth Dock, you will find **Maryport Steamships**, where you can learn all about Maryport's shipbuilding industry. Take a tour round the VIC96 where you can have a go at raising and lowering sails on a Brigantine model, learn how to tie ship's knots and even climb into a sailor's hammock! Step onto The Flying Buzzard and find yourself back in the 1950's with a running commentary bringing to life this former pride of the Clyde Shipping Company's Tug Fleet. Here you can visit the engine room and discover how The Buzzard worked and why she sank.

Dearham, about two miles inland from Maryport, though not a pretty village, has a very beautiful church with open countryside on three sides.

The chancel is 13th century and there is a fortress tower built for the protection of men and beasts during the Border raids. Standing 4ft high is the Adam Stone, dating from AD900, depicting the fall of man, with Adam and Eve hand in hand above a serpent. There is also an ancient font carved with mythological beasts, a Kenneth Cross showing the legend of the 6th-century hermit brought up by seagulls, and a magnificent wheel-head cross, 5ft 4in high, carved with 'Yggdrasil', the Norse Tree of the Universe.

The Old Mill Inn   Dearham   0900 813148

Enjoying a quiet location in the centre of Dearham, you will find **The Old Mill Inn,** so named because part of the building dates back to the 17th century and used to operate as a corn mill. The interior is particularly attractive with unusual painted panes of glass throughout, which feature brightly coloured flowers, butterflies and birds. Run by Angela Greenwood, this charming pub offers an extensive and imaginative menu, which includes such delights as Salmon en Croute with Broccoli Sauce, Spinach and Mushroom Lasagne, and Chewy Fudge Brownie Cheesequake. The Old Mill Inn also provides accommodation in seven tastefully co-ordinated guest rooms, two of which are en-suite and all with TV and hot drinks facilities.

Nearby **Bridekirk,** just north of Cockermouth, is well worth visiting for its church which contains one of the finest pieces of Norman sculpture in the coutry, a carved font with runic inscription and a mass of detailed embellishments. It dates from the 12th century and the runic inscription states it was made by 'Richard'. He is shown on one side with a chisel and mallet. Not only is this a superb example of early English craftmanship, but it is exceedingly rare to find a signed work. Ancient tombstones stand round the walls of the cruciform church and inside it has unusual reredos (a wall behind the altar) of fleur-de-lys patterned tiles.

Little Broughton and **Great Broughton** on the River Derwent, south-east of Maryport, were communities involved in weaving and pipemaking. Further downstream is **Camerton**, whose old, grassed-over slag-heaps are the only evidence of its coal-mining origins. Camerton is set in a particularly lovely section of the wooded Derwent Valley with the panorama of the Lakeland Fells as a backcloth. In the small and ancient church stands a memorial statue of 'Black Tom', the famous warrior Thomas Curwein, who died in 1500.

Eaglesfield was the birthplace of Robert Eaglesfield, who became confessor to Queen Philippa, Edward III's Queen. He was also the founder of Queen's College, Oxford where he was buried in 1349. More famous is John Dalton who was born here in 1766. The son of Quaker parents, Dalton was one of the most brilliant scientists, naturalists, and mathematicians of his age and was the originator of atomic theory. A memorial now marks his house. He taught at the village school at the age of 12, before going to Manchester to follow his remarkable scientific career.

Cockermouth is a Cumbrian market-town which has retained its unspoiled character, less overrun by tourists than its neighbours to the west. There are pleasant shops and restaurants along a busy main street set against a majestic backdrop of fells. Wordsworth was born here and his old home in Main Street, which has been at various times a shop, a cobbler's and a tearoom, was the National Trust's first Information Centre, a function which it still retains. Now known as the Wordsworth House, it was built in 1745 and retains its original staircase, fireplace and fine plaster ceilings. There are some personal effects of the poet and you can visit his childhood garden.

Another famous son of Cockermouth was Fletcher Christian, the man who led the mutiny on 'The Bounty'. He was born in 1764, at Moorland Close, a farm about a mile south of the town, and attended the same school as Wordsworth.

Beatfords   Cockermouth   0900 827099

Cockermouth Castle dates from the 13th and 14th centuries but is not open to the public. Part of it was built with material from the Roman Fort 'Derventio', at Papcastle, immediately north-west of Cockermouth. It has had an eventful history; it was besieged by Robert the Bruce and saw action in both the Wars of the Roses and the Civil War.

Tucked up a little walkway off the main street in Cockermouth, in Lowther Went Shopping Centre, you will find **Beatfords**, a delightful country restaurant and tea rooms. Open daily from April to October and Monday to Saturday the rest of the year, this attractively decorated licensed establishment offers both a daytime and evening menu. During the day you can choose from a vast selection of speciality teas and coffees accompanied by a range of home-made cakes and light snacks. In the evening, the mouthwatering menu offers such delights as Cheesy Prawn Pots, Chicken in Rum, and a variety of Steak dishes, followed by a wide selection of freshly made sweets such as sticky toffee pudding and fresh fruit ice-creams.

Two miles from Cockermouth lies the picturesque village of **Tallentire** where you will find a lovely 17th century pub, **The Bush Inn**. Pretty hanging baskets adorn the entrance and there is a warm friendly atmosphere inside, where you will soon find yourself feeling at home as you have a drink and a chat with the locals. Host Alan Wilkie provides excellent bar meals six days a week, both at lunchtime and in the evening. The menu is extensive and varied with something to suit every palate, including a wide range of vegetarian dishes and an above average children's menu. With the large food portions and nice selection of accompanying wines, a meal at the Bush Inn is a real treat.

The Bush Inn   Tallentire   0900 823707

From Cockermouth town centre if you follow the B5292 south for 2 miles you will come to a crossroads. Turning right here, then left after 150 yards, down a 'No Through Road', you will arrive at **Stanger Farm**. Enjoying a beautiful location with the River Cocker running alongside, this is a working dairy farm run by a friendly couple, Carolyn and Robin Heslop and guests are welcome to watch Robin milking the cows. Inside the house you will find very comfortable accommodation in two tastefully decorated double bedrooms, with a large lounge area downstairs and a cosy dining room where Carolyn serves her large farmhouse breakfast. This is a substantial meal which ensures you will never leave Stanger Farm feeling hungry!

Loweswater, which can only be reached by narrow lanes, is one of the smaller of the lakes, in an enchanting fell-side and forest setting. From Cockermouth, take the B5292 and at Lorton, the B5289, turning off to Brackenthwaite, after which you will come to Loweswater village. A public bridleway which takes you around the far side of the lake, whose name, appropriately, means 'leafy lake'. You can return along a quiet lane at the far side and there is a car park near Waterend.

Stanger Farm   Cockermouth   0900 824222

North of Loweswater is one of the quietest and least-known parts of the Lake District National Park, a group of low fells through which there are few roads or even paths, summits such as Fellbarrow, Smithy Fell, Sourfoot Fell. The little river Cocker divides this group from the Lorton Fells, further east, forming the Beautiful Vale of Lorton.

Lorton is a village in two parts. Low Lorton has a pele tower and **Lorton Hall** is reputed to be haunted by a woman carrying a lighted candle. There are also two priest holes. The Scottish King Malcolm III (1057-93) stayed at the Hall with his Queen on a visit to the southern part of his Kingdom of Strathclyde - at that time part of Scotland.

High Lorton, about half a mile away, has a village hall known as Yew Tree Hall where the Quaker George Fox preached to Cromwell's soldiers. The yew tree that stands nearby inspired Wordsworth's famous poem which begins, *'There is a yew tree, pride of Lorton Vale....'.*

Gilbrea Farm   High Lorton   0900 85256

Irving and Marjorie Blamire are a hardworking, friendly farming couple who offer a warm welcome to all visitors coming to their charming

257

home **Gilbrea Farm** at High Lorton. The farmhouse is situated on the road over Whinlatter Pass to Cockermouth and enjoys a peaceful location with magnificent views of the Buttermere Fells. This is an ideal place for those wishing to stay on a working farm, and is well situated for walking, climbing, and exploring the beautiful Lake District countryside. This is a non-smoking establishment with accommodation in two very comfortable family rooms, and a large farmhouse breakfast provided each morning. Whilst Marjorie does not supply an evening meal herself, she will happily recommend some good places to eat.

From High Lorton a steep road travels east through the thickly forested Lorton Fells, over the Whinlatter Pass to Braithwaite, to Derwent Water and Bassenthwaite Lake.

From Lorton and beyond Brackenthwaite, the B5289 skirts the edge of Crummock Water and continues to Buttermere. The walk around Buttermere gives superb views. One of the great scandals of the 19th century involved Mary Robinson, the Beauty of Buttermere, who thought she had married the Earl of Hopetoun's brother, only to discover that in fact her husband was a bankrupt imposter. He was hanged and she later married a local farmer.

Derwent Lodge Hotel   Embleton   07687 76606

Situated between Keswick and Cockermouth, in the lovely village of Embleton, you will find **Derwent Lodge**, a beautifully converted 18th century farm building which offers top class hotel accommodation. Surrounded by magnificent Lakeland scenery, the hotel's terraced lounge boasts superb views across the valley towards Mount Skiddaw and Bassenthwaite Lake. The accommodation is excellent, with 11 en-suite bedrooms and the luxury of a sauna, spa bath and solarium. Refreshed, you can sample some of the local brews in the cosy lounge bar followed by dinner in the comfortable restaurant. Open to non-residents, it offers

258

a first class table d'hote menu accompanied by a comprehensive wine list. To complete your stay, there are also various sporting and leisure activities available nearby ranging from golf to pony trekking.

Low Hall Country Guest House Brandlingill 0900 826654

Further on and tucked away in a secluded corner of the Western Fells at Brandlingill, **Low Hall Country Guest House** is a first class non-smoking establishment run by Enid Davies. This charming 17th century farmhouse stands in two and a half acres of beautiful countryside with a stream running through the grounds. The accommodation comprises six guest rooms, all en-suite and tastefully decorated, whilst downstairs you can relax in one of the two lounges, with a roaring log fire in the winter. Meals are taken in the beautiful beamed dining room, with a choice of breakfast dishes available and, in the evening, the highlight of your stay is a candlelit dinner with an imaginative and varied menu prepared by Enid, accompanied by a carefully selected wine list.

The north-west corner of Cumbria, overlooking the Solway Firth dividing England and Scotland, is perhaps the least-known part of this beautiful county. And yet it is an area rich in heritage, with a network of quiet country lanes, little-frequented villages, old ports and seaside resorts along a coast which is full of atmosphere.

For centuries **Wigton** has been the centre of the business and social life of the Solway coast and plain, its prosperity based on the weaving of cotton and linen. It has enjoyed the benefits of a Royal Charter since 1262 and a market is still held on Tuesdays. Today most of the old town is a Conservation Area and if you look carefully along the Main Street, you can see how the upper storeys of the houses have survived in an almost unaltered state. On street corners, metal guards to prevent heavy horse-drawn waggons damaging the walls, can still be seen. Not to be missed is the magnificent Memorial Fountain in the Market Place, its gilded, floriate panels set against Shap granite and summounted with a golden cross. It was erected in 1872 by George Moore, a 19th-century philanthropist, in memory of his wife Eliza Flint Ray, with whom he fell in love when he was a penniless apprentice. Bronze reliefs show four of her favourite Charities - giving clothes to the naked, feeding the hungry, instructing the ignorant and sheltering the homeless. The figures were carved by Thomas Woolner, a pre-Raphaelite sculptor. Just above the town is Highmoor Tower, a local landmark built by two eccentric but wealthy brothers, William and Edwin Banks, to house a large bell and a carillon of eight smaller ones.

It's a pleasant drive of some seven miles across the coastal plain to **Newton Arlosh** on the Solway marshes. The village's name comes from 'the new town on the marsh' and it was first established by the monks of Holm Cultram Abbey in 1307 after the old port at Skinburness had been destroyed by the sea. Work on the church did not begin till 1393, but the result is one of the most delightful examples of a Cumbrian fortified church. In the Middle Ages there was no castle nearby to protect the local population from the Border raids and so a pele tower was added to the church. The narrow doorway measures 2ft 7in and the 12in, arrow slot, east window makes it the smallest in England. After the Reformation, the church became derelict but was finally restored in the 19th century. Inside, there is a particularly fine eagle lectern carved out of bog-oak.

Abbeytown, as its name suggests, grew up around the 12th-century Abbey of Holm Cultram on the River Waver and many of the buildings are constructed of stone taken from the abbey when it fell into ruins. The village is small, little more than a hamlet, surrounded by ancient farms in a rolling landscape of lush meadows. Founded by Cistercians in 1150, the Abbey bore the brunt of the constant feuds between the English and the Scots. In times of peace the community prospered and soon became one of the largest suppliers of wool in the North. Edward I stayed here in 1300 and again in 1307 when he made Abbot Robert De Keldsik a member of his Council. After Edward's death the Scots returned with a vengeance and in 1319 Robert the Bruce sacked the Abbey, even though his own father, the Earl of Carrick, had been buried there 15 years earlier.

The final blow came in 1536 when Abbot Carter joined the Pilgrimage of Grace, the ill-fated rebellion against Henry VIII's seizure of Church lands and property. The rebellion was put down with ruthless brutality and the red sandstone church of St Mary survived because local people pointed out that it was the only building strong enough to provide protection against Scottish raiders. It is still the parish church and was restored in 1883, a strange yet impressive building with the original nave shorn of its tower, transepts and chancel. The east and west walls are

Drinking fountain

Village water pump

Chemist sign

The Tiny Bridge House, Ambleside

heavily buttressed and a porch with a new roof protects the original Norman arch of the west door. Within the church buildings is a room, opened by Princess Margaret in 1973, which contains the gravestones of Robert the Bruce's father and that of Mathias and Juliana De Keldsik, relations of Abbot Robert. There are some lovely walks along the nearby River Waver which is especially rich in wildlife.

Silloth is an old port and a seaside resort well worth exploring. Its promenade provides wonderful views of the Solway Firth and the coast of Scotland. The town centre is made particularly attractive by thirty six acres of grassy, open space known simply as 'The Green'.

With the coming of the railways in the 1850s, Silloth came into being as a port and railhead for Carlisle. The Railway Company helped to develop the town, and had grey granite shipped over in its own vessels from Ireland to build the handsome church which is such a prominent landmark. The region's bracing air and low rainfall made Silloth a popular seaside resort. Today it remains a delightful place to stroll, to admire the sunken rose garden, the pinewoods and two miles of promenade. The 18-hole golf course was the 'home course' where Miss Cecil Leitch (1891-1978), the most celebrated woman golfer of her day, used to play. Another famous woman player was the great contralto, Kathleen Ferrier, who stayed in the town for part of her tragically short life.

Find time if you can to drive or walk up the coast to Skinburness. In the Middle Ages Skinburness was a lively market town and was used by Edward I in 1299 as a base for his navy when attacking the Scots. A few years later a terrible storm destroyed the town and what survived became a small fishing hamlet. It's well worth the short walk along the two mile spit of land, **Grune Point**, the start of the Allerdale Ramble, to view the great estuary and the beautiful, desolate expanse of marshland and sandbank. Grune Point once contained a long-vanished Roman fort, but now forms part of a designated Site of Special Scientific Interest because of the variety of its birdlife and marsh plants.

In the opposite direction from Silloth, further down the coast, is the village of **Beckfoot**. At certain times and tides, the remains of a prehistoric forest can be seen on the sand-beds. To the south of the village is the site of a 2nd-century Roman fort known as 'Bibra'. According to an inscribed stone found here, it was once occupied by an Auxiliary Cohort of 500 Pannonians (Spaniards) and surrounded by a large civilian settlement. Look out for the small stream flowing into the sea which was used in World War I as a fresh water supply by intrepid German U-boats. There is also a Quaker meeting house (now a private house) and a graveyard dating from 1735.

This part of Cumbria was a Quaker stronghold in the 17th and 18th centuries and in Old Mawbray, a village of whitewashed cottages two miles further south, the first Quaker marriage was held in great secrecy amongst the sandhills.

Holme St Cuthbert, a hamlet a couple of miles inland, is also known as Rowks because in the Middle Ages there was a chapel here dedicated to St Roche. The present church dates from 1845, but contains an interesting torso of a medieval knight wearing chain-mail. It was found by schoolboys on a nearby farm, the hollowed-out centre being used as a trough. It seems to be a 14th-century piece and could be a statue of Robert the Bruce's father who died at Holm Cultram Abbey. North-east of the hamlet, and enveloped among low hills, is a lovely 30-acre lake known as Tarns Dub which is a haven for birdlife.

The headland of Dubmill Point is popular with sea-anglers. When the tide is high and driven by a fresh westerly wind, the sea covers the road with lashing waves. Spray is often sent down the chimney of an old farm which was built on the site of a former water corn-mill belonging to the abbey of Holm Cultram.

Just to the south is **Allonby**, which has a history as a sea-bathing resort in the 18th century and it still keeps much of its Georgian and early Victorian charm with cobbled lanes, alleyways and some interesting old houses. It was also an important centre for herring fishing and some of the old kippering houses can still be seen.

Coach House Swiss Restaurant   Whitehall   09657 388

Lanes lead from here to **Bromfield**, where there was a wooden church in the 2nd century. Its stone replacement stands on the site where St. Mungo (the affectionate name for St. Kentigern) came in AD670. Close by he sank a well which is still there, capped by a stone cover, and still used by villagers for christenings.

Aspatria lies on the main A596 road immediately above the shallow

Ellen Valley. For most visitors its main interest is the elaborate memorial fountain to 'Watery Wilfred', Sir Wilfred Lawson MP (1829-1906), a lifelong crusader for the Temperance Movement and International Peace. The much-restored Norman church is entered through a fine avenue of yew trees. It contains some ancient relics which include a 12th century font with intricte carvings, a Viking hogback tombstone and a grave cover with a pagan swastika on it. Like many other churches in the area, the churchyard contains a holy well in which it is said St Kentigern baptised his converts.

Not far from Aspatria, the delightful **Coach House Swiss Restaurant** lies at the end of long tree-lined driveway at **Mealsgate**, close to the junction of the B5299 and the A595 Cockermouth to Carlisle road. This impressive 50-cover restaurant is situated on the ground floor of a Grade I listed sandstone coach house which was constructed in 1862 as part of the Whitehall Estate. Proprietors Ueli and Audrey Maeder offer a menu of imaginative dishes, many of which are served with delicious Swiss sauces and dressings. They are also able to cater for small parties and functions. The restaurant is open daily except Tuesdays and non-Bank Holiday Mondays. Ueli and Audrey also have two beautifully appointed ground-floor holiday apartments available all year round, situated at the rear of the building leading on to a quiet cobbled courtyard.

The village of **Gilcrux** on the other side of the River Ellen, between Aspatria and Cockermouth, has particularly good views to Scotland and it is well worth visiting for the little village church of St Mary that stands on a walled mound, with a buttressed exterior, thick-walled chancel and a hagioscope.

So with Scotland in our sights, we must now leave this beautiful corner of the country and hope that you have enjoyed your "journey" with us. We are most grateful for the kindness and hospitality shown to us during our time researching the area and we are sure the places featured would be pleased if you mention that "The Hidden Places" prompted your visit.

And finally, in the words of the great Lakeland poet Wordsworth:

"Persons of pure taste throughout the whole island, who, by their visits (often repeated) to the Lakes in the North of England, testify that they deem the district a sort of national property, in which every man has a right and interest who has an eye to perceive and a heart to enjoy."

Tourist Information Centres

ALSTON, Alston Railway Station, Tel: (0434) 381696

AMBLESIDE, Church Street, Tel: (05394) 32582

APPLEBY-IN-WESTMORLAND, Boroughgate, Tel: (07683) 51177

BARROW-IN-FURNESS, Duke Street, Tel: (0229) 870156

BOWNESS-ON-WINDERMERE, Bowness Bay, Tel: (05394) 42895

BRAMPTON, Market Square, Tel: (06977) 3433

CARLISLE, The Old Town Hall, Tel: (0228) 512444

COCKERMOUTH, Market Street, Tel: (0900) 822634

CONISTON, Yewdale Road, Tel: (05394) 41533

EGREMONT, Main Street, Tel: (0946) 820693

GRANGE-OVER-SANDS, Main Street, Tel: (05395) 34026

GRASMERE, Red Bank Road, Tel: (05394) 35245

HAWKSHEAD, Main Car Park, Tel: (05394) 36525

KENDAL, Highgate, Tel: (0539) 725758

KESWICK, Market Square, Tel: (07687) 72645

KILLINGTON LAKE, Road Chef Service Area, M6 Southbound,
Tel: (05396) 20138

KIRKBY LONSDALE, Main Street, Tel: (05242) 71437

KIRKBY STEPHEN, Market Square, Tel: (07683) 71199

LONGTOWN, Memorial Hall, Tel: (0228) 791876

MARYPORT, Senhouse Street, Tel: (0900) 813738

MILLOM, St. Georges Road, Tel: (0229) 772555

PENRITH, Middlegate, Tel: (0768) 67466

POOLEY BRIDGE, The Sqaure, Tel: (07684) 86530

RAVENGLASS, Railway Station, Tel: (0229) 717278

SEATOLLER, Seatoller Barn, Tel: (07687) 77294

SILLOTH-ON-SOLWAY, The Green, Tel: (06973) 31944

SOUTHWAITE, M6 Service Area, Tel: (06974) 73445

ULLSWATER, Main Car Park, Tel: (07684) 82414

ULVERSTON, County Square, Tel: (0229) 57120

WATERHEAD, Car Park, Tel: (05394) 32729

WHITEHAVEN, Market Place, Tel: (0946) 695678

WINDERMERE, Victoria Street, Tel: (05394) 46499

WORKINGTON, Washington Street, Tel: (0900) 602923

Visitors travelling from the south should call in at the 'Gateway to Cumbria' TIC at Pavillion Motorway Services, Forton on the M6 between Junctions 32 and 33:
FORTON, M6 Service area, Tel: (0524) 792181

Town Index

W

Y

NOTES

NOTES

NOTES

NOTES

NOTES

NOTES

NOTES

NOTES

NOTES

NOTES

THE
HIDDEN PLACES

If you would like to have any of the titles currently available in this series,
please complete this coupon and send to:

M & M Publishing Ltd
Tryfan House, Warwick Drive
Hale, Altrincham
Cheshire, WA15 9EA

Somerset, Avon and Dorset	☐	£ 5.90 inc. p&p
Norfolk and Suffolk	☐	£ 5.90 inc. p&p
Yorkshire	☐	£ 5.90 inc. p&p
Devon and Cornwall	☐	£ 5.90 inc. p&p
	☐	£ 5.90 inc. p&p
Cumbria	☐	£ 5.90 inc. p&p
Southern and Central Scotland	☐	£ 5.90 inc. p&p
Sussex	☐	£ 5.90 inc. p&p
Hampshire and the Isle of Wight	☐	£ 5.90 inc. p&p
Gloucestershire & Wiltshire	☐	£ 5.90 inc. p&p
Nottinghamshire, Derbyshire & Lincolnshire	☐	£ 5.90 inc. p&p
Oxfordshire, Buckinghamshire & Bedfordshire	☐	£ 5.90 inc. p&p
Lancashire & Cheshire	☐	£ 5.90 inc. p&p
Hereford & Worcester	☐	£ 5.90 inc. p&p
Set of any Five	☐	£ 25.90 inc. p&p

NAME..

ADDRESS..

....

...............................Post Code...

Please make cheques/postal orders payable to: M & M Publishing Ltd